# Contents

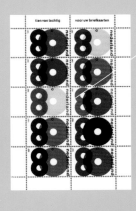

# V&A

# Contributors

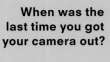

When was the last time you got your camera out?

Film or digital?

Who would take your fantasy portrait?

**MELANIE MUES** is not just a designer.

**Yesterday.**

Digital, but boy do I miss my 35mm film rolls.

Diane Arbus. Weird and wonderful.

**MAX LEONARD** is a writer recovering from tax panic.

**Cycling with the Fireflies Ride in the Alps, to accompany a diary for a magazine.**

Film. Unfortunately. I don't take many photos since I got a digital camera—instant gratification spoiled the fun, as it tends to.

Lartigue. He looked fun.

**SCOTT KING** is a designer.

**Two weeks ago— I was feeling guilty about lying on a beach when I should have been working, so I tried to turn lying on a beach into a 'project'.**

Digital, they say.

Brian 'Brit Pop' Sweeny assisted by Cecil Beaton.

**LAURA CLAYTON** is a freelance writer and stylist.

**Yesterday. My cat enjoys contorting himself into the most insane, unfeline poses and it's impossible to resist documenting them.**

Film. I usually have a Polaroid, Diana or Lomo LCA in my bag.

I wouldn't mind travelling back to the 1920s for a bit of surreal, soft-focussed Madame D'Ora treatment. Although having now met him, it would have to be the amazing Jason Evans.

**JAMES LANGDON** is designing a big book.

**Most days, usually photographing dusty old books at the library to later hunt for in online secondhand shops. Latest find: Three Dimensional Structures of Wood (An Ultrastructural Approach), 1976.**

Digital.

Don't mind who takes the picture. Would be nice if Hans-Peter Feldman found it on the street though.

**NICOLE JACEK** is a designer.

**If my iphone counts, then eleven hours ago.**

Digital.

My friend Ella Smolarz. She is weird.

**JASON JULES** is a creative consultant, stylist and writer.

**I took a picture of a tea mug designed by Mandi Martin for Pellici's Cafe to post on my blog (garmsville. blogspot.com)**

I shoot digital, but if I was good enough I'd shoot film.

My favorite living photographers are: Nigel Christian, Tim and Barry, Tyrone Lebon, Ben Rayner, Yamandu Roos, Kofi Allen and Tribble & Mancenido. A portrait by any of those guys would be make me happy.

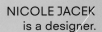

# Print Matters Part 1 Environmental Policy Guide Part 2 Standard Paper Guide (FSC/ Recycled)

# Available soon

team

# Things to See and Do

# Animal Magic

Charlotte Dumas takes intimate but unsentimental portraits of animals, some domestic, some working and some in captivity, but all under man's spell in some way. A new exhibition entitled Paradis (which runs at the Foam Gallery in Amsterdam) brings together her various series for the first time — there are horses, wolves, tigers and bears taken on Dumas's travels across the States and Europe. Shots include stray dogs in New York and Palermo, tigers in Texas and Indiana, army horses and race horses in Paris. Through her revealing yet understated shots, Dumas examines the complex and often touching relationship between man and animal.

www.foam.nl

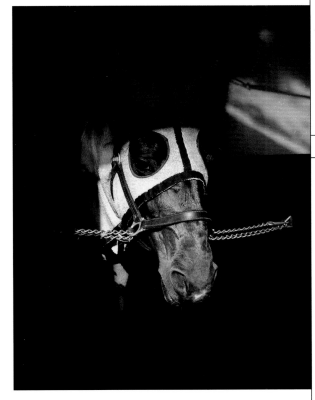

SEPTEMBER

# Fashion Forward

17 SEPTEMBER—20 DECEMBER

Can it really be nine whole years since photographer extraordinaire Nick Knight's SHOWstudio.com burst onto our computer screens? However did we mange without it? This month sees the groundbreaking website's first major retrospective at Somerset House, showcasing many of the pivotal projects made with its merry band of high-profile photographers, models, artists, writers, designers, stylists and assorted hangers-on. Arranged around three themes – Process, Performance and Participation – the exhibition will look at what happens when the often seemingly opposing worlds of fashion and film collide.

www.showstudio.com

# Book Club

25—27 SEPTEMBER

If you haven't already been to visit the fantastic new-look and very tastefully extended Whitechapel Gallery, this could be just the excuse you need. The London Art Book Fair has relocated there this year and promises to be an unmissable event. Designed by Established and Sons and Foreign Office Architects, there will be over eighty exhibitors – as well as the major art-book publishers, and museum and gallery publishing houses, there's a chance to meet independent artist bookmakers and publishers and university presses. Grayson Perry and Martin Parr will be talking and signing; and you can even take a crash bookbinding workshop courtesy of the Society of Bookbinders.

www.whitechapelgallery.org

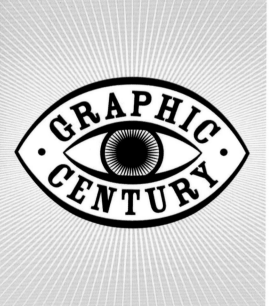

## Pop Life

01 SEPT–3 OCT

Contrary to what some people believe, appreciating art doesn't have to include suffering. If you like your art on the uplifting side, then why not take a trip down to Beaux Arts in London's Cork Street for some light relief in the form of David Spiller's irreverent interpretations of classic pop lyrics. A riot of colour, Spiller effortlessly mixes cartoon characters, flowers and typography to create canvases that are energetic and irreverent.

www.beauxartslondon.co.uk

## Top Form

19 SEPTEMBER—14 OCTOBER

If you're in the Los Angeles area, why not check out the stunning imagery and excellent draughtsmanship of Hellovon, who has his first solo show at the Cerasoli Gallery in Culver City this month. The show is called Semblance, which is also the title of one of the artist's ongoing projects. As well as many brand-new pieces, the show also features drawings from his acclaimed Animal series, which appeared on billboards in London and then New York, and was subsequently adopted by Liberty of London for its relaunch.

www.cerasoligallery.com

## Zero Gravity

9—13 SEPTEMBER

Onedotzero launches its thirteenth annual festival at the BFI Southbank this month with a jam-packed schedule that promises to both entertain and inspire by the bucketload. As well as old favourites such as Wow + Flutter (which features short films) and Wavelength 09 (showcasing music videos), other highlights include a H5 retrospective and the UK premiere of its amazing short film Logorama, a preview of Alistair Siddons' breakdancing movie Turn It Loose, an animation workshop for kids and the first public screening of Disney's new animated blockbuster UP, in glorious 3D.

www.onedotzero.com

# London Design Festival

19—27 SEPTEMBER

It's September in London and we all know what that means — loads of black-clad/skinny-jeaned designery types, endless private views and many, many sachets of Resolve. Yup, it's the London Design Festival — back, bigger and busier than ever (it now encompasses 100% Design and London Fashion Week) and with quite a few top-notch graphic design-related events this year (makes a nice change, 'eh?). Here's Grafik's pick of the best…

www.londondesignfestival.com

# Mag Culture

11 SEPT—31 OCT

Typographer Herbert Spencer's seminal Typografica is widely touted by self-appointed design critics as one of the most important design magazines to have appeared in the post-war period. Although it was published over a nineteen-year period between 1949 and 1967, only thirty-two issues were printed in total, making it virtually impossible to get hold of a copy these days. You can get all hot under the collar while perusing the full set (along with various enlarged spreads) at the Kemistry Gallery this month, in an eponymously titled exhibition organised by 'Uncle' Rick Poynor.

www.kemsitrygallery.co.uk

# Sporting Chance

22—24 SEPTEMBER

Curated by your favourite graphic design magazine and celebrating the rich relationship between graphic design and the Olympics, some of the UK's most talented graphic designers have created an original poster based on each of the thirty-nine Olympic sports and disciplines. It would be unfair to single out any contributor, as the list reads like a Who's Who of the UK graphic design community. The limited-edition posters and accompanying catalogue will be for sale, and profits will be donated to children's sports charity Right to Play and the UK Paralympic Fund. Why not buy a whole set?

www.grafikmag.com/olympik

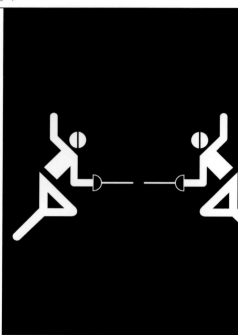

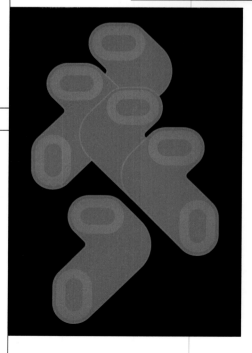

# Danger Zone

19 SEPT—08 OCT

London Transport has an amazing track record for commissioning graphic design — its poster archive represents one of the most extensive collections of British graphic design history. During this year's LDF the museum is holding an exhibition entitled The Outer Limits — Beyond Zone One, showcasing the winning entries to its recent competition to design a poster for the Underground singing the joys of Greater (as opposed to Central) London. In true democratic fashion, the competition was open to anyone and the show acts as a nice precursor to the museum's major exhibition on Suburbia which opens next month.

www.ltmmuseum.co.uk

-KEEPS LONDON GOING

# Culture Shock

22 SEPTEMBER, 6—8PM

An exciting new graphic design publishing venture launches during this year's LDF. Unit Editions is the brainchild of graphic design archduke Adrian Shaughnessy and Spin's Tony Brook, Studio Culture is its first publication and you're all invited to the book launch at the trendy Haunch of Venison gallery in Mayfair. Providing a unique glimpse into nearly thirty leading graphic design studios, it promises to reveal the secret life of the studio "laid bare with disarming frankness." Ooo-err, we can't wait. Maybe it should have been called Graphic Design Babylon instead?

www.uniteditions.com

# Out There

19—27 SEPTEMBER

A brand-new graphic design initiative held at Rich Mix in Bethnal Green and curated by Fraser Muggeridge and set up to support recent graduates launches at this year's LDF, entitled Emerge. Don't let the dodgy logo put you off. The very worthwhile event gives graduates the chance to showcase their portfolios, meet established designers and challenge them to a poster design-off to win the coveted Emerge graduate design award. What's more, every graduate in the country will have the opportunity to showcase their work via a massive postcard wall installation as well as taking part in lots of useful portfolio critiques and workshops.

www.e-merge.info

CandyLab Ltd, 130 Shaftesbury Avenue, London W1D 5EU. Tel: 020 7031 0888

Created for CIA / Weiden + Kennedy

At CandyLab we use hard science to make sweet dreams, creating beautiful, unforgettable images in two and three dimensions. Because we cleverly manage your assets across all the different medias. For more information please visit www.candylab.co.uk

*CandyLab*.co.uk

Make imaginary sweeter

# Rasmus Svensson

Swedish hardcore chiller and Kevin Costner fan Rasmus Svensson keeps a pineapple on his desk for inspiration and plans to make – then lose – a lot of money, preferably by designing an energy drink can. His new-age-meets-1980's design style is as quirky as his ambition…

01

02

01 From the series Globes, published in Futureclaw magazine, Spring 2009

02 Spread from Hus, saker & manniskor, published 2009

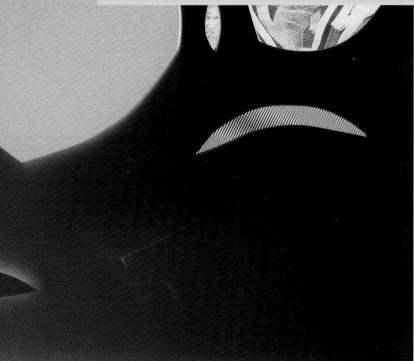

03

02

01 From the series
Compositions, 2009

02 03 From the series Globes,
published in Futureclaw
magazine, Spring 2009

**Describe your style in three words.** — Gradients, drop shadows, bad eye-hand coordination.

**What materials do you use to make your illustrations?** — All kinds of stuff. Mostly pencils, paper, paint and computers.

**Where do you find inspiration?** — In cyberspace, old books, food and forgotten blockbusters.

**Who are your heroes?** — Andy Kaufman.

**What's the best thing about your town?** — Gothenburg is an ocean city full of hardcore chillers who are down for whatever. There are lots of hills, so you always have a good view.

**What's been the best and worst reaction to your work?** — The worst reaction is total indifference. The best reaction is a lifelong friendship.

**Describe your workspace to us.** — I have a white table with a pineapple on it. On the wall there is a triptych of photographs of flower arrangements and a screenprint by the talented Y. Val Gesto. The table is right next to the fireplace. On the mantlepiece I keep my collections of rocks and minerals.

**What would be your fantasy commission?** — Designing the can for an energy drink.

**What's the best creative/art space near to where you live?** — Well, the best art space in Sweden is without a doubt the gallery called Krets in Malmö. All kinds of stuff happens there. Crazy stuff.

**What first got you into design?** — I got into doing visual things through music. Doing record covers and show posters. After a while the design part grew to be at least as important as the music. They balance each other well.

**How much do you use the internet in publicising your work/ what methods of getting people to see your work do you use?** — I put a lot of my work on the internet, and use the internet and its various subspaces for communicating with people. But I also trade a lot of physical things (such as zines, posters, records, tapes) with people by old-fashioned mail. My philosophy on publicising is, to quote Kevin Costner in Field of Dreams, "If you build it, they will come."

www.rasmusemanuelsvensson.com

# Some design flaws you can hide. Others need a more creative approach.

Get a bigger box of tricks.
Cherry Illustration. Only at Veer.com

# Lucy Barlow

Who says that sitting in a cupboard and talking to a mannequin's hand as a child can't lead to success later on in life? For some it's the perfect prelude to an existence filled with poetry, art and wet dreadlocks, as artist Lucy Barlow is finding out…

01 Fire Ladders, watercolour
and pastel on sugar paper, 2009

02 Bears say NO, ink on paper, 2009

03 Bloom, oil on paper, 2009

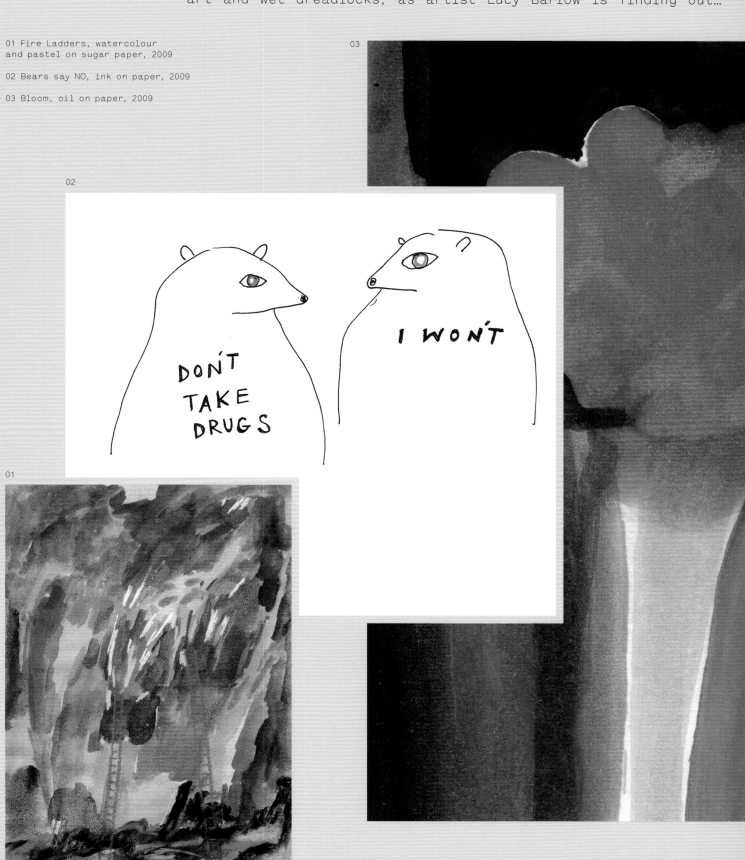

01 Pass Me a Biscuit, graphite
and crayon on paper, 2008

02 Untitled II, watercolour
and chalk on paper, 2009

03 Odessa, acrylic on paper, 2008

04 Connie, oil on paper, 2009

**Talent** Lucy Barlow

**Describe your style in three words.** — Mellifluous, soft, seeking.

**What materials give you the most pleasing results?** — Oil on fine, old paper. Dip-pen and black ink scratching a surface. Oil laid down on bits of wood—old doors, floorboards, cheese boxes. Anything that I can be quite forceful or near-violent with. I like to strip back, reveal.

**Where do you find inspiration?** — Inspiration exists everywhere. Tops of trees jangling in the breeze, an escapee dreadlock on a pavement, Greek yoghurt in the heat, wet withered roses, sounds of sleeping animals. I could go on for days… And love in all its shapes. That's the big one.

**Who are your heroes?** — Matisse makes me shiver, Warhol makes me want to keep going when it's tough, all of my friends and family. Can Nature be my hero/heroine too?

**Tell us a secret technical trick.** — It's an oldie, I stole it from Mr Hockney: adding washing-up liquid to acrylics—sheeny smooth.

**What's been the best and worst reaction to your work?** — If somebody wants to own a piece of my work, that is a wonderful reaction. I love it, too, when people stop and really take time to look at the work. The worst reaction was when I overheard a woman talking about my "carrot dangling from a ceiling beam on piece of ribbon over a plate of honey" installation at Modern Art Oxford, only because, for a second, it made me think "what on earth am I doing". Thankfully, that moment only lasted for a moment.

**What's the best advice you've ever been given?** — Be yourself, as good as you can be. Do not try to emulate those that you admire, draw your inspiration from them, but channel it. Be you—there is only one you.

**What would be your fantasy commission?** — Anything for the Guggenheim, New York. I wholeheartedly adore the space. Or a collaboration with Louise Bourgeois on Primrose Hill. She fascinates and excites me with her brilliance. Why Primrose Hill? No idea. Just think it would be lovely to make something with her there. Something phallic, gentle, gushing upwards towards the sky. Something you could see from way over yonder. Mm mm.

**What first got you into painting?** — I have always painted, and drawn. When I was a little girl I would keep myself to myself in a big cupboard in my bedroom, just drawing and making up stories, talking to a mannequin's hand my mother gave to me from her job as a window dresser. I loved mark-making. I still do. I started taking painting seriously after I visited New York and saw some incredible work over there. It opened up my eyes wide, made me realise how important painting is to me, and how I needed to give myself over to it.

**What's next for you?** — An art fair soon in London, which should be exciting (my first), a group show in Camberwell in September, and another group show in an Oxford gallery early next year, and, of course, lots and lots of beavering away. It never stops. I never want it to.

www.lucybarlow.net

Grafik Presents
Olympik

39 Sports
39 Designers
39 Posters

A selling exhibition
with proceeds donated
to Right To Play and
Paralympics GB

22 — 24
September 2009

German Gymnasium
6 Pancras Road
London
NW1 2TB

Grafik
Team Impression
GF Smith

grafikmag.com/ok

Design
SEA

Laurenz Brunner
**The Most Beautiful Swiss Books 2008**

James Langdon
**Simon and Tom Bloor**

Christopher West Your Message Here

Tomato **The Lea Shores**

DesignStudio **Centrefold**

# Showcase

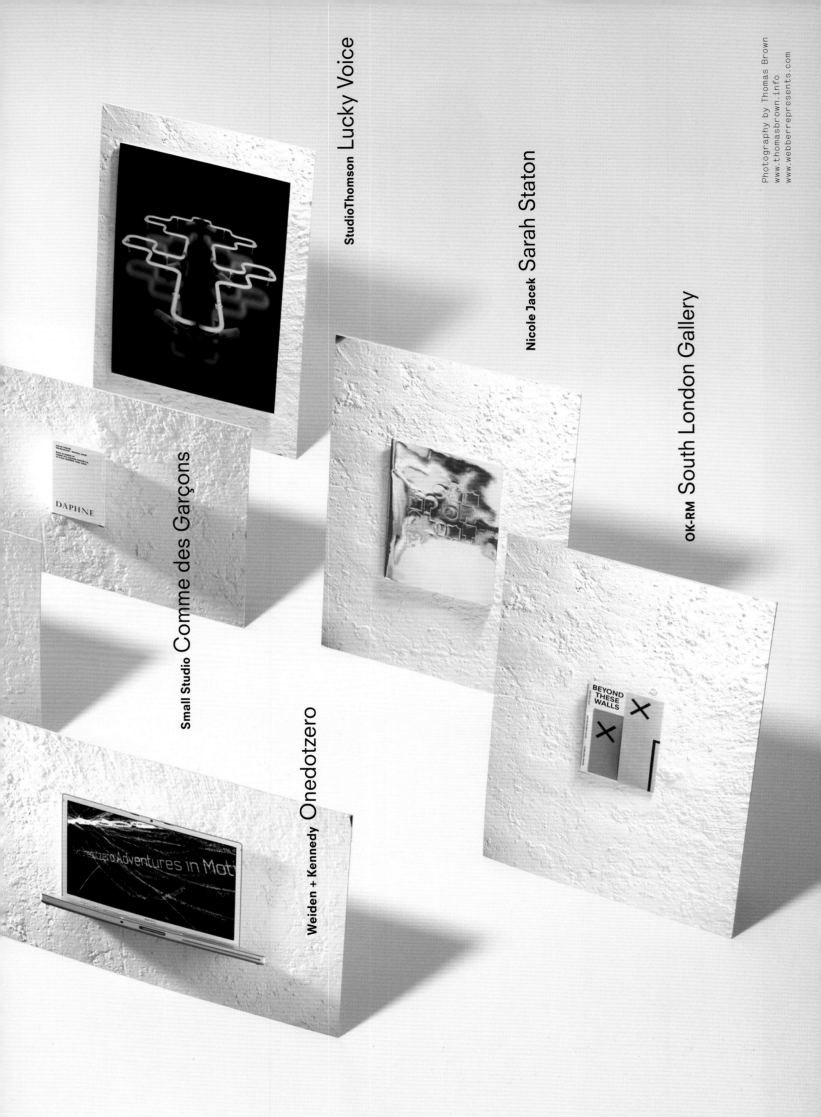

StudioThomson Lucky Voice

Nicole Jacek Sarah Staton

ok-RM South London Gallery

Small Studio Comme des Garçons

Weiden + Kennedy Onedotzero

DAPHNE

BEYOND THESE WALLS

Adventures in Motion

Photography by Thomas Brown
www.thomasbrown.info
www.webberrepresents.com

## Tomato The Lea Shores

It's been fifteen years since Dylan Kendle and Jason Kedgley (now reunited at the Tomato studio) last worked together on a record sleeve design. They've collaborated in other media but not a drop of vinyl has passed between them since the Underworld album Second Toughest in the Infants came out in 1994 in the early days of Tomato.

That's all changed with South London psychedelic band The Lea Shores and a new limited-edition box set to mark the release of its debut album.

Kendle has a refreshing, simple, rock 'n' roll verve to his passion for sleeve design. There is no mention whatsoever of the digital revolution and how great graphic design can save dwindling record sales, just pure joy at a job well done. Kendle recounts the story: "The Lea Shores had been unable to secure a major record deal so, after securing some venture capital to record their album, they decided to put it out themselves, no expense spared… well, not quite, but pretty good considering, so we used incremental die-cuts, coloured vinyl and debossing."

The design is fairly minimal: at first glance the box appears to be just a black box, bringing to mind a "none more black" Spinal Tap moment, but on opening the box the detail is there, as Kendle explains: "Jason Kedgley and I have a shared love of Op Art and like a stripped-back aesthetic."

The forty-five-degree incremental die-cuts are one of the outstanding features. As Kendle explains: "It nodded to the exclusivity of the package. I remember vinyl imports having a forty-five-degree cut and them feeling extra-special. Secondly it works as a functional device to get the sleeves out of the box and, thirdly, it introduces colour phase and depth. The band were very amused to be paying me to cut corners."

www.tomato.co.uk
www.myspace.com/theleashores

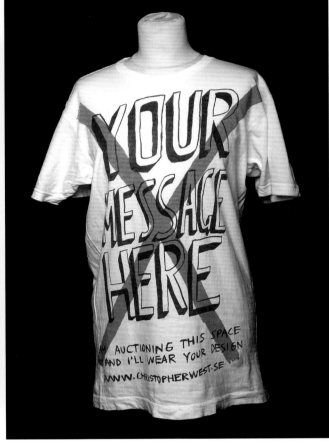

## Christopher West Your Message Here

The Gerrit Rietveld Academie in Amsterdam is a remarkable place; there's no doubt that it's one of the most respected art colleges in the world. The loyalty and love that the students have for the place is quite staggering. Little wonder, then, that, when all is dandy, the authorities decide to throw the proverbial spanner in the works and relocate the students to another building away from their beloved 1960s space. The debate rages on and the graphic design students have found themselves busy creating posters and manifestos; there's nothing like political upheaval to drum up a bit of business.

Graduating this year, Christopher West came up with a novel business plan and performance based on print. "All I knew when I started was that I wanted to work with repetitive actions and create a body of work around it. I wanted to print one T-shirt every week and decided to wear it for seven days. It was

also important to me to reach outside of Amsterdam." A space on a white T-shirt was sold on eBay every week; the winner of the auction was then obliged to design a message that West printed and wore for seven days before the process was then repeated with a new T-shirt. The entire collection was then displayed at the graduation show before being sold off one by one at an auction in the college. Needless to say, many of the students took the opportunity to create their own political slogans in defence of the college staying put at its current site. "I guess I was in the right place at the right time," West muses. "But I'll learn to live in another environment now." Will future students at the Rietveld have to do the same? The story continues.

www.your-message-here.com

# DesignStudio Centrefold

SEA, BB Saunders and Spin have all guest-edited Centrefold, the much-sought-after fashion and photography magazine by Andrew G. Hobbs. This time, for the fourth issue, it's the turn of DesignStudio, based in East London. DesignStudio is a newcomer. As Paul Stafford says: "We haven't been around very long and that in itself was a very good reason for taking on this project. Centrefold is a great calling card, as the pedigrees of previous designers, and the other collaborators, the fashion designers, photographers and sponsors, are all so good."

DesignStudio worked alongside photographers from Webber Represents, photographer and editor Andrew G. Hobbs and guest editor Georgina Hodson. Seven photographers were featured in the issue, including Alexandra Catiere, Alan Clarke, Thomas Brown and Tim Simmons. The result is a sixty-four-page publication limited to an edition of 1,000 copies – it's so popular within the fashion industry that all copies are requested by clients before they can be distributed and sold.

Stafford explains the design rationale: "We wanted to re-establish and reinforce the design concept of the centrefold idea. The magazine is folded and created in such a way as to allow each issue to be folded round the next; also the centrefold idea allows for large-scale, full-bleed photography. We reintroduced the dynamic crops of previous issues through the use of folds. By using the folds to create section dividers which contain the titles and credits, we have allowed for an uninterrupted flow of imagery from cover to cover."

Centrefold's print production was handled by G&B Printers and the paper was supplied by GF Smith, tying up the collaboration very neatly. Andrew G. Hobbs certainly has a great eye for match-making. It's a magazine that's too popular to make money – quite an accolade.

www.wearedesignstudio.com
www.centrefoldmagazine.co.uk

**Laurenz Brunner**

# The Most Beautiful Swiss Books 2008

When Lars Müller is interviewed by Laurenz Brunner and Tan Wälchli in The Most Beautiful Swiss Books 2008, he says: "What I have realised for quite a few years now is that the best talents of this country go abroad as soon as they can. They may come back later but with more international experience, which then re-influences the Swiss scene." He could have been talking directly about Brunner himself. A Swiss national, Brunner was educated at Central Saint Martins in London before settling in Amsterdam to teach at the Gerrit Rietveld Academie. Brunner is yet to return permanently to the fold, but his input as the designer (with Tan Wälchli) for the 2008 edition of this Swiss Federal Office of Culture-sponsored book is certainly a homecoming of sorts.

Every year, around thirty books are awarded with an exhibition at the Museum of Design in Zurich and the Mudac in Lausanne. Brunner was given the challenge of creating the catalogue of this year's selection. The book is divided up into sections: an immensely readable jury interview with Lars Müller, Linda Van Deursen, Paul Neale and Cornel Windlin, which sheds light on contemporary thinking in Swiss design; essays by Rob Giampietro and David Reinfurt, James Goggin, Cynthia Leung, Lisette Smits and Tan Wälchli. It's a wonderfully idiosyncratic publication, slightly schizophrenic in its delivery, a mixture of textbook, catalogue and promotion. Lars Müller sums up his view: "I have realised that one could divide beautiful books up into two categories, those that are beautiful in terms of utility, of instrumental quality, and those that are more luxurious." The book that Brunner has designed falls firmly into the first camp.

www.laurenzbrunner.com

## Small Studio Comme des Garçons

The Hon Daphne Guinness and Comme des Garçons have joined noses and produced a limited-edition perfume. They chose Small Studio to produce the artwork. David Hitner at Small Studio, with the assistance of Spencer Wallace at Nirvana Creative Solutions, came up with some print solutions that reflected the product and managed to implement an innovative use of materials as well. Hitner picks up the story: "We produced a number of visuals, which were discussed with Daphne and Adrian Joffe, Comme des Garçons' president. We decided on a crisp white bookcloth-covered box with a high-gloss, deep black interior. The perfume bottle inside, a traditional-shaped bottle with an etched logo, was to be contained within a deep red velvet bag to represent a heart."

The real innovation came into play as a result of tests based on the logo being reproduced in traditional foil block technique used for hardback books. After much experimentation it became apparent that this was not going to produce the quality they wished to achieve. Hitner had recently been shown a new product by Justin Hobson at Fenner Paper — a litho-printable bookcloth. As Hitner explains: "[The material] was very new to them and had never been used for packaging or printed with such fine, detailed type. Nirvana engineered a series of tests for us using various techniques and different ink compositions before arriving at the one used on the final packaging."

The resulting packaging fits snugly into the Comme des Garçons stable, while giving off a suitable air of aristocratic whimsy. What does Daphne smell like? With bitter orange from Sicily, incense and saffron, Indonesian patchouli, amber and vanilla from Madagascar, we'd say absolutely delicious.

www.studiosmall.com
www.doverstreetmarket.com

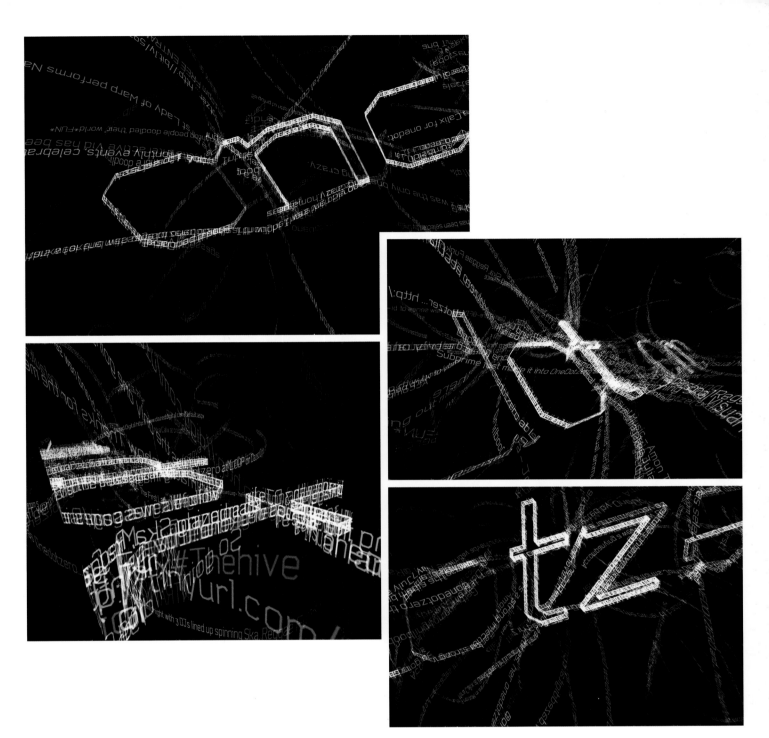

## Weiden + Kennedy Onedotzero

onedotzero is a vast sprawling media enterprise these days. It's therefore no wonder that when Shane Walters, creative director and CEO of onedotzero, got together with Weiden + Kennedy to come up with this year's brand identity for the Adventures in Motion event at the BFI, the result was themed around "convergence and collaboration". David Bruno of Weiden + Kennedy explains the thinking: "We looked at how we could harness the community and decided to use online conversations to create the identity. We gathered the live dialogue from Twitter and Facebook and channelled the content via specially produced software, devised by Karsten Schmidt, through streams that then form the logo and font of onedotzero's name."

Walters is enthusiastic about the project. "Every year we commission a piece of work," he says, "and it's great to be able to tie in the branding with something that can also be an installation. We are planning to project the artwork in the space during

the event and people will be able to input their own communication. There is an amazing buzz around onedotzero and it's good to see that communication being put to creative use."

Adventures in Motion is still some way off (it will be staged in November) but plans are already afoot for the installation. Bruno is keen to point out that the software is open source and that that's part of the concept — that there should be an atmosphere of sharing connections rather than ring-fencing technology. "I like the fact that it's organic," he says. "It's been an interesting challenge for us, but a good one. A lot of our clients see us as purely an advertising agency; we want to be known as an ideas agency and this will go some way towards that." We quite agree.

www.wklondon.com
www.onedotzero.com

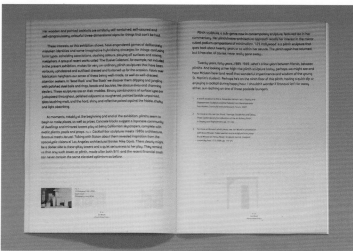

## Nicole Jacek Sarah Staton

Nicole Jacek shines and so does her work. Producing an accompanying identity and catalogue for Sarah Staton's latest exhibition, Transformations 2: A Clump of Plinths, at the Lowry in Salford, Manchester, allowed Jacek the opportunity to sparkle even more. However, as she says, "There was a little problem; the choice for the cover appeared not to be the most affordable material on the planet."

The solution to the budgetary conundrum came with a two-colour print on pink paper with a four-colour section of photographs by Jonty Wilde and Ben Blacknell on white matte paper for the inside of the catalogue. This meant Jacek could splash out on a radiant opal mirrorboard cover – "a fluid approach to highlight Sarah's candy-like pop artwork."

This is the second time Jacek has collaborated with Staton. They met while Jacek was working for Ian Anderson at the Designers Republic. Jacek worked on a catalogue for Staton entitled Shucks, Sucks, Sticks, Stucks and the relationship blossomed from there.

Making the connection between Jacek's design and Staton's artworks, Jacek created a new font – "little sculptures," as she says, "ready for mass production, just as god intended." The result is a great marriage of eccentric, idiosyncratic candy pop.

When asked about the inspiration behind the work, Jacek has plenty of ammunition to hand. "Words for Sarah and her art that pop into my mind are: Pop Art, female Damien Hirst, glamorous, hyper-reality, intelligent, lovely, funny, crazy, serious, honest, mind-blowing, crafts and British. The catalogue had to express and implement all these characteristics."

The exhibition runs until 6 September and the catalogue is available at Walther Koenig Books, Charing Cross Road, London and the Yorkshire Sculpture Park Shop.

www.nicolejacek.com
www.sarahstaton.com

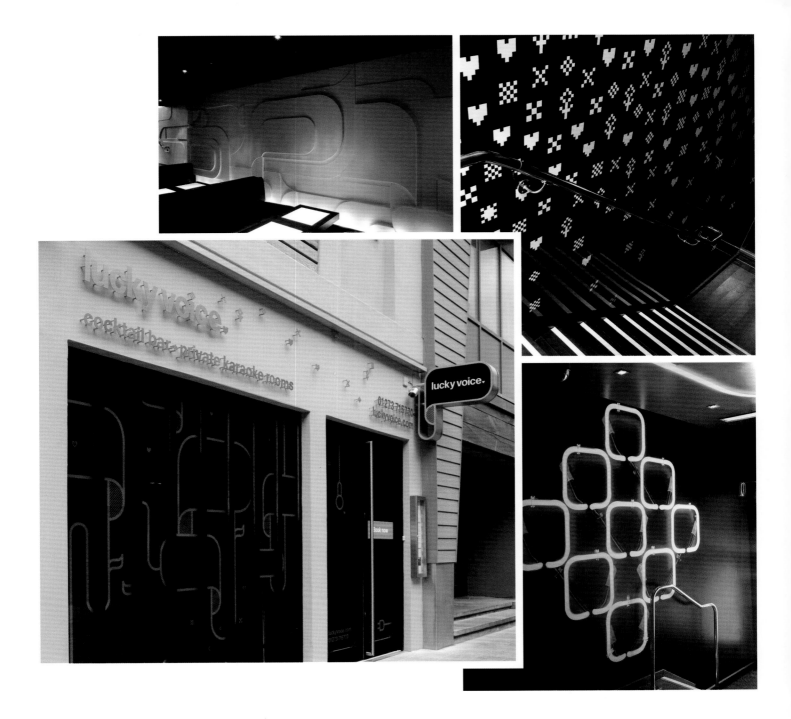

## StudioThomson Lucky Voice

When French engineer Georges Claude harnessed the sexy, sleazy cocktail of noble gases and created coloured neon in a glass tube in 1910, little did he know that he'd be changing the way we advertised fast food, musical entertainment and prostitution for ever. Lucky Voice is an emporium that deals in musical entertainment, an upmarket chain of karaoke bars owned by Martha Lane Stewart, the dotcom success story who made a fortune with Lastminute. com. Lucky Voice's branding was originally created by MadeThought, but for its latest venture — a venue in Brighton — it has brought in StudioThomson to oversee the interior design. This is a first for the studio as its output has, up until now, been print-based. Mark Thomson explains: "Our creative concept was to bring the existing brand icons to life as brightly coloured neons to capture the excitement, energy and live performance aspect of the karaoke experience."

Studio Thompson had five neons manufactured, and commissioned photographer Louisa Parry to photograph them in various set-ups. Architects Julian Taylor Design Associates worked with the studio on exterior and interior design to implement the neon theme across the entire building.

The photographic montages were printed as large-scale, wide-format digital wallpaper and installed throughout the venue. The neons themselves were enclosed in Perspex boxes and used as part of the front reception desk, and also in the corridor on the second floor. In addition to the digital wallpaper, the project also involved the design of all interior and exterior signage, as well as bar details such as seat stitching and a wall relief based on the existing branding.

If he were around today Georges Claude would surely approve, and who knows, he may even have belted out a verse or two of Je Ne Regrette Rien.

www.studiothomson.com
http://bars.luckyvoice.com

Simon & Tom Bloor
As long as it lasts

Opening 20 February 7 to 9pm

21 February to 4 April 2009
Thursday 12 to 7pm
Friday & Saturday 12 to 5pm

# Better A Broken Arm

# Than A Bruised Spirit

Eastside Projects
86 Heath Mill Lane, Digbeth
Birmingham B9 4AR
www.eastsideprojects.org

Eastside Projects is a new artist-run space
as public gallery for the city of Birmingham

Eastside Projects is a not for profit company
in partnership with Birmingham City University
and revenue funded by Arts Council England

Simon &
Tom Bloor

As long
as it lasts

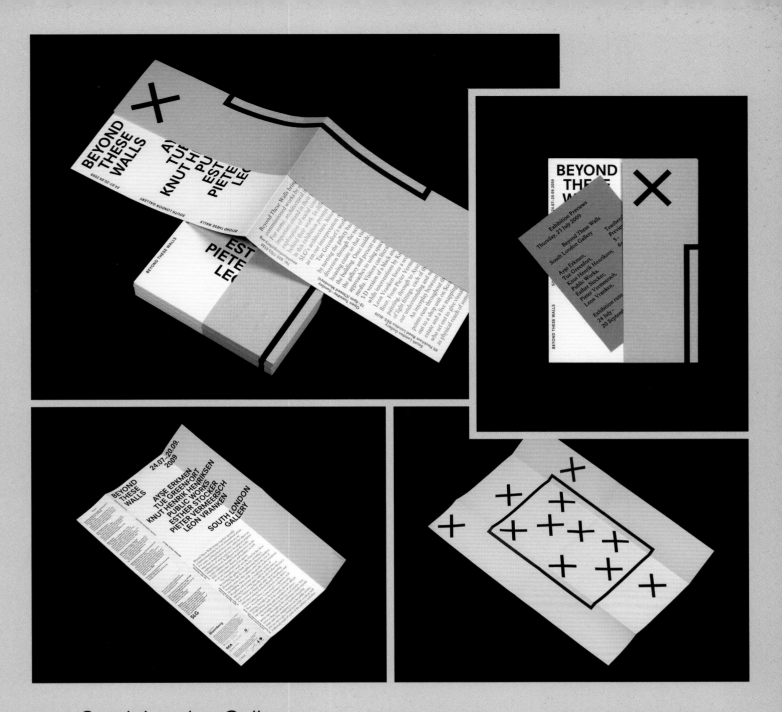

## OK-RM South London Gallery

Oliver Knight and Rory McGrath of OK-RM were commissioned by Sangeeta Sathe, marketing and communications manager at the South London Gallery, to come up with the identity for Beyond These Walls, an exhibition of architectural interventions both inside and outside the gallery space. Sathe commissioned the pair on the strength of their work for the Harvard Art Museum in Boston, Massachusetts in 2008 and perhaps also for their self-professed penchant for design "organised around a principle." There is also a link between the Harvard Art Museum's desire to portray architectural transformation with Beyond These Walls' own ambition to "transform the gallery and present an inspiring variety of approaches to using space."

Knight and McGrath took the concept of the exhibition and ran with it. "The brief was more of a discussion really," explains McGrath, "and the resulting artwork is more a diagram of the exhibition concept." The design is simple and tight; the flip-side of the flyer is an illustrative, non-geographical, map where each of the artworks

on display is marked by an 'X'. Each further piece of collateral material, the invitation and the press release are variations on this theme, creating a visual language devised by Knight and McGrath. The notion of 'inside and out' is carried through to the paper fold, deliberately overlapping and drawing attention to the boundaries between the exterior and interior of the flyer. The identity for the museum also extends to signage, which the gallery was keen to see used outside the traditional areas of the space, again blurring the lines to highlight the concept.

With the design following the artistic concept, the resulting artwork can be seen as a creative extension of the exhibition. There may be seven international artists listed but there is an honorary design duo that deserves an artistic credit as well.

www.ok-rm.co.uk
www.southlondongallery.org

# KAREL MARTENS

Portrait of Karel Martens
by David Bennewith (Colophon)

The benevolent grandfather of graphic design, Karel Martens observes the magic and wonder of language, mathematics and colour and then translates them into design classics. ANGHARAD LEWIS and ROBERT URQUHART went to meet the man who's given so much to the world and yet still remains very much in awe of it.

# WEEKOVERZICHT

"I see the alphabet as a miracle—twenty-six characters and you can make them do so many different things. There is no one page in all the books in the world that is the same—not even one line—that's unbelievably fascinating for me."

01 Monoprint, from an ongoing series of uncommissioned work and printing experiments, 1960 - now. Stencil numbers printed letterpress in a 'magic' formation, as found in Vedic mathematics. The series reads both left to right and top to bottom. After 10, the number is found by adding together its two digits. Thus 15=1+5=6.

02 Beatrix coin for Ministry of Finance, The Hague, 1998

Anybody—especially a designer—could learn a lot from Karel Martens. As well as being a very experienced teacher (he has been teaching graphic design since 1977 and co-founded—and still runs—Werkplaats Typographie, the very well-respected Masters course for typography in the Netherlands), Martens' way of working, his way of living and the symbiosis of life and work in his designs seem a parable in motion. Martens is seventy years old but still full of genuine wonder about things that less curious souls take entirely for granted—he finds numbers endlessly fascinating, the alphabet is "a miracle" and the fact that you can make any colour out of just three primary colours is "magic."

Many Grafik readers will be familiar with Printed Matter, the book that was published to celebrate his winning the Dr A.H. Heineken Prize for Art in 1996. It is considered something of a classic in the world of design publishing and rare copies (only 4,000 were printed) sell on eBay for jaw-dropping sums. Such adulation as the graphic design community is apt to bestow on certain designers is often at odds with the unassuming nature of the 'legends' themselves. The Karel Martens who warmly welcomes us into his studio in Amsterdam and who, after the interview, goes off down the road waving to us from his bicycle, is a wonderfully human legend.

As the jury's introduction to Printed Matter puts it, "his work is characterized by workmanship and simplicity. He is not one for glamour." In Martens' studio on the water in Amsterdam, we find an industrious set-up. In a bright, high-ceilinged room there are workbenches, a coat stand for his printer's jacket and a huge wall covered in collected ephemera, and he is busy making preparations for the end of term at Werkplaats. Tomorrow there will be the last few interviews for this year's intake and he and James Goggin, the newest addition to the Werkplaats staff, will make the final decision on which ten or twelve prospective students will join the prestigious course in the autumn.

Werkplaats applications come from all over the world. Martens runs through his current students individually by name—there are people from the UK, Brazil, the Balkans, Belgium, Korea, USA, Australia and the Netherlands. The students often feed in from other design schools in Europe and commonly they have already been working professionally as designers. At the Werkplaats studio everyone—both students and teachers—brings in real commissioned projects for real clients. This has been a part of the way Werkplaats has been run since Martens founded it with former student Wigger Bierma in 1998 (more recently he has worked alongside Armand Mevis) with the aim of responding to what they saw as problems in the existing model of design education in the Netherlands. At Werkplaats Martens wasn't interested in churning out identikit 'professionalised' designers, but rather in giving students space and time to develop their own interests and find a personality as a designer.

He draws on his own experience as an art school student in the early Sixties. "I'm not educated as a designer," he points out. "I started my practice in 1960 and at that time graphic design didn't exist. I was in an art school [Arnhem School of Art] where I was educated for five years and there were a lot of disciplines—painting, sculpture-making, all sorts of classes—and only one day a week they mentioned illustration and publicity. The teacher was a fine artist. It was a very nice time." So there is a balance sought in the Werkplaats educational model between personal expression and practical application. These play out against a background of discussion and of enquiry into the world beyond design. "A little bit what I'm regretting now in design education," Martens continues, "[is that] it's design, design, design, the students always looking in magazines, looking at how other designers are doing it—it's incestuous… Students often see inspiration in copying things, not in the energy of [the work] or the mentality behind the design but the flavour [of it] and the superficial work."

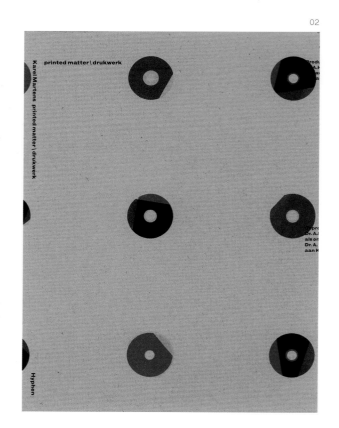

01 The wall in Karel Martens'
studio (detail) by David Bennewith

02 Cover of Printed Matter, published
on the occasion of Martens winning
the Dr A. H. Heineken Prize for Art
in 1996

03 04 Architectural Positions, poster
and catalogue spreads (designed with
Aagje Martens), for a series of six
seminars on 'Architecture, Modernity
and the Public Sphere', TU Delft, 2007

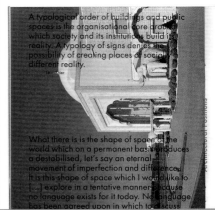

Monumentality and Public Representation

A typological order of buildings and public
spaces is the organisational core around
which society and its institutions build its
reality. A typology of signs denies the
possibility of creating places of social
different reality.

What there is is the shape of space of the
world which on a permanent basis produces
a destabilised, let's say an eternal
movement of imperfection and difference.
It is this shape of space which I would like to
[...] explore in a tentative manner because
no language exists for it today. No language
has been agreed upon in which to discuss

Thursday 12/04/07, 18:00 – 21:00
Faculty of Architecture, TU Delft, Zaal A

Introduction
Deyan Sudjic

Until the advent of modernity, the monumental character of
public structures was more or less an established constant.
A public building, after all, had to reflect, or even uplift, the
people. The pre-eminent and imposing aspect of theatres,
city halls and libraries furnished city dwellers with an identity,
and there were specific codes or typologies that elevated
the architecture of the public building above its surroundings.
Modern architects, however, seem less comfortable with
monumentality. The codes for imposing palaces, churches
and city halls proved obsolete. Yet architecture seems never
to have fully broken free of monumentality; public buildings,
after all, still require a certain recognisability.
  In contemporary architecture, monumentality remains a
sensitive subject, which only a few architects have dared to
address. Hans Kollhoff, for instance, overtly seeks buildings
that can structure the city and connect to a specific monumental tradition. This monumentality, in Kollhoff's view, is necessary for the city to be liveable and recognizable. A few
other contemporary designers demonstrate, however, that
monumentality does not necessarily coincide with a classical
architectural idiom. The work of Jean Nouvel, for example, is
intensely monumental: buildings that dominate their surroundings in a prominent way and have a very significant impact
on the experience of visitors. An architect such as Peter
Eisenman, on the contrary, seeks a less explicit formal idiom.
If public space is an expression of the people, Eisenman
argues, contemporary architectural practice must take into
account a society who is no longer monolithic. A monumental
architecture, according to Eisenman, is an architecture that
represents mutability and diversity.

Introduction
Deyan Sudjic

Architecture critic. He was visiting
professor at the Royal College of Art
in London and editor of Domus, the
international magazine of art, architecture and design. He was Director
of the Venice Architecture Biennale
in 2002. At the moment he is director
of the London Design Museum.
His latest book, The Edifice Complex
(2006), was a seminal contribution to
the debate on the main theme of this
seminar.

Position 1
Bernard Tschumi

Architect and educator. He has
taught, amongst others, at the
Architectural Association in London,
Princeton University and Columbia
University, where he was also Dean.
Bernard Tschumi is a prominent contributor to the public
sphere. In this perspective some of his
most well-known publications are
The Manhattan Transcripts (1994),
Event-Cities (1994, 2000, 2005)
and Bernard Tschumi: Conversations
with Enrique Walker (2006).

Position 2
Hans Kollhoff

Architect. He has been running
an architectural office with Helga
Timmermann since 1984. Since
1990 he has been Professor of
Architecture and Construction at
the ETH in Zurich. His projects in
Germany and the rest of Europe
have been primarily in office,
business and residential construction.
Important publications concerning
the main theme of this seminar are
'Stadt Ohne Tradition?' (1994),
'Against the Taboos of an Urban
Architecture' (1995) and Hans
Kollhoff: Architektur/Architecture
(2003).

Apr 12    4    Monumentality and Public Representation

03

# Spring 2007/ Faculty of Architecture/ TU Delft

**Architectural Positions**

| | | | |
|---|---|---|---|
| **02.07** | **Changing Definitions of Public & Private** | | **1** |
| Introduction | Position 1 | Position 2 | |
| Richard Sennett | Manuel de Solà-Morales | Rem Koolhaas | |

**Architectural**

| | | | |
|---|---|---|---|
| **03.01** | **The Themporalities of the Public Sphere** | | **2** |
| Intro | Position 1 | Position 2 | |
| René Boomkens | Bernard Tschumi | Willem Jan Neutelings | |

| | | | |
|---|---|---|---|
| **03.15** | **Image Building and Public Space** | | **3** |
| Intro | Position 1 | Position 2 | |
| Lieven de Cauter | Léon Krier | Michiel Riedijk | |

| | | | |
|---|---|---|---|
| **04.12** | **Monumentality of the Public Representation** | | **4** |
| Intro | Position 1 | Position 2 | |
| Deyan Sudjic | Rem Koolhaas (ov) | Hans Kollhoff | |

**Positions**

| | | | |
|---|---|---|---|
| **04.26** | **Alternating Programs and Practices** | | **5** |
| Intro | Position 1 | Position 2 | |
| John Habraken | Antonio Monestiroli | Antonio Monestirolli | |

**Architectural**

| | | | |
|---|---|---|---|
| **05.04** | **The Perception of the Public** | | **6** |
| Intro | Position 1 | Position 2 | |
| Juhani Pallasmaa | Steven Holl | Lars Spuybroek | |

1, 2, 3, 4, 5, 6 In het voorjaar van 2007 organiseert de afdeling 'Architecture and Modernity; Public Building' van de Faculteit Bouwkunde van de TU Delft een reeks symposia rondom het thema architectuur-moderniteit-publiek domein onder de titel 'Architectural Positions'. Op een zestal middagen wordt gepoogd een aantal architectonische debatten die rondom dit thema hebben plaats gevonden te 'reconstrueren' door enkele posities in dit debat te illustreren en daarmee ook te ac-tualiseren.

Thursdays/ Room B/ 18:00 – 21:00

**TUDelft**

Seminars on Architecture, Modernity and the Public Sphere

04

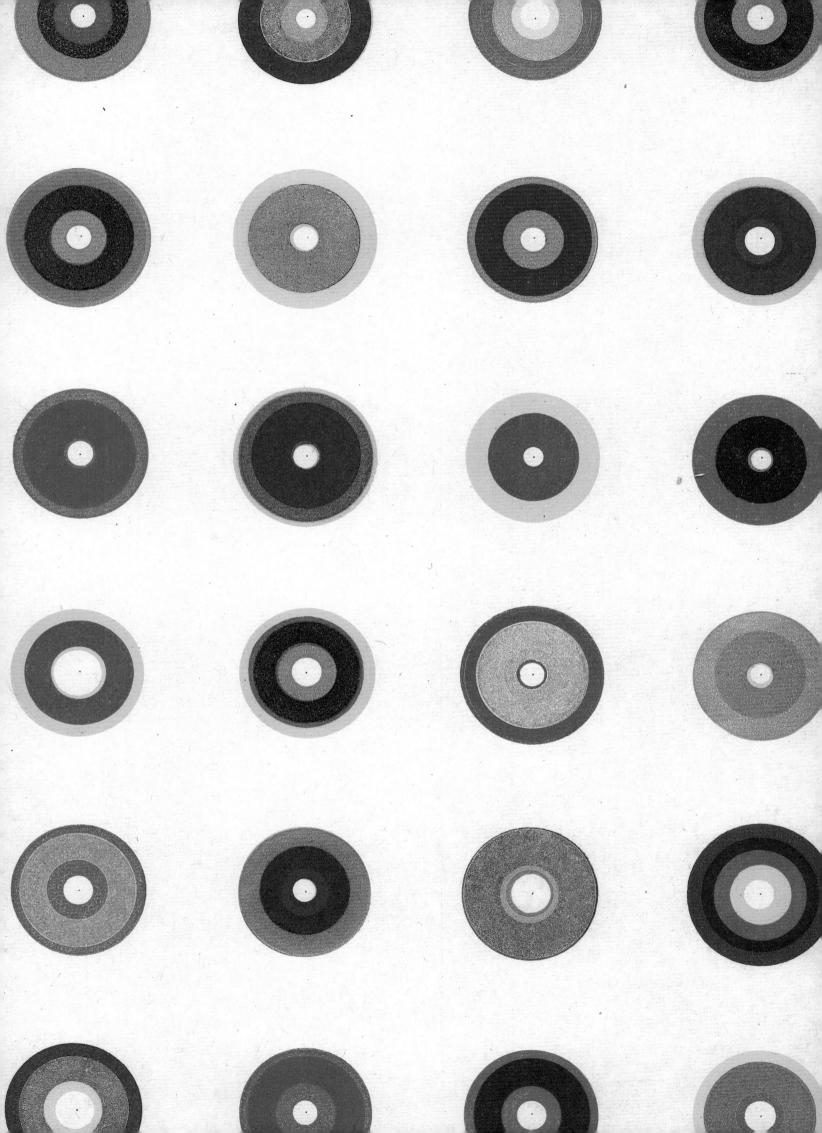

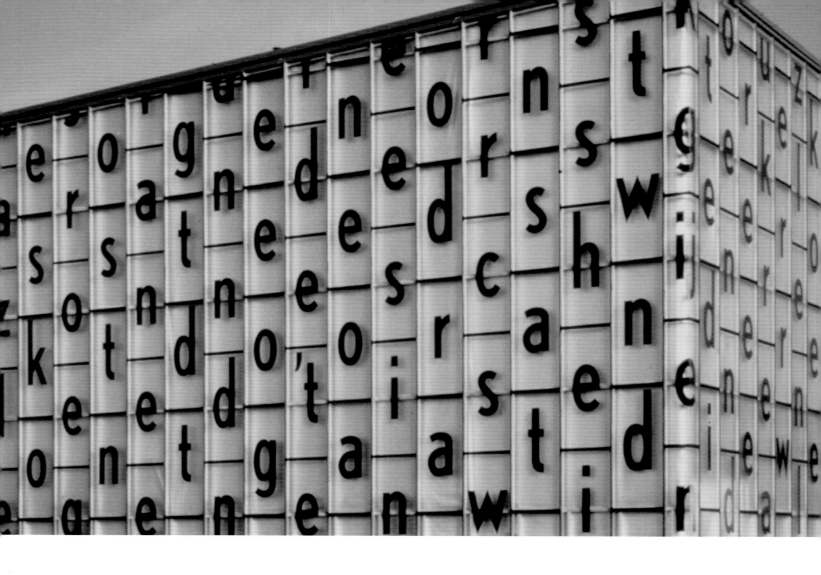

So an awareness of design is something to be mindful of but not reliant upon—as you see when you look at Martens' own work: it is not design movements or trends that stimulate him, or find their way into his work, but fundamental things about the world and how we make sense of it, such as language, mathematics and colour. In turn, Werkplaats students are encouraged to seek their own sources of wonder with which to fuel their practice. "Our school is not, in a way, about celebrating design, it's more discussing design," Martens says. "I see tradition and convention more as a reference—I see design as not only questioning design, but also questioning the tradition and the convention."

When Martens launched the workshop (as part of postgraduate education within the ArtEZ Institute for the Arts in Arnhern), he also had his studio based on the campus. One project that he has consistently shared with successive groups of students is the design of OASE, the architectural journal founded by the students of Delft University of Technology in the early 1980s, and which Martens has been designing since 1990, when he dispensed with a standardised logo, instead creating an entirely new visualisation of the word 'OASE' on the cover of each issue, directly based on its content. This somewhat rebellious design approach was significant to Martens in 1990. "This magazine is a kind of dialogue with the contributors," he tells us. "For me this is very important: I'm from a modernist background and, as you know, in the beginning that was always working with a grid, and using Helvetica and every company had the same logo and colours—a kind of uniformity. For me [OASE] was a good reason to break from the uniformity of the modern movement, although I still believe in the modern movement but not all aspects. So I started without a logo."

There is a short text by Martens in Printed Matter entitled "What design means for me" and within this he writes about the role of the graphic designer: "Graphic designers act as intermediaries… There is always talk of a given message (the job) and of the one who is to be informed (the public). Between them stands a designer with a specific outlook and knowledge of things. For good things to happen there has to be a dialogue, with mutual respect, between the client and the designer." Martens places great import on the relationship with the client or the commissioner in the 'game' of design. As well as teaching this relationship in the most practical way at Werkplaats, Martens has a rich history of relationships with clients—many long-standing—where discussions about the design of a project have advanced the form in which he presents the content. One of the biggest companies Martens has worked for is the Dutch PTT Telecom company, for which he designed a series of telephone cards in 1994. "It was an ideal job," Martens recalls. The rectangular, widely distributed, pocket-sized format would make the now-obsolete phone card something of a dream job for any designer, rivalled only by stamps or coins (both of which Martens has also designed). "The PTT office for design had very good people and good commissioners at that time," he recalls. After he submitted his initial ideas, however, a committee rejected his proposals and he had to go back to the drawing board and develop them a bit further. This was no bad thing though, as he sees it: "Designers can be arrogant so actually I see it that commissioners are part of the deal. I always see the commissioner as a valid person— a good commissioner is very important. If a commissioner just says everything's okay all the time that sometimes makes designers a little bit lazy."

Previous page left:
Monoprint, from an ongoing series
of uncommissioned work and
printing experiments, 1960–now

Previous page right: Façade for
Veenman Printers Ede printworks,
commissioned through Neutelings
Riedijk architects, featuring
a poem by K. Schippers, 1996.
Each of the 1460 units contains
one letter (using Nobel typeface).
Photo by Daria Scagliola

This page: Selection of covers
for OASE magazine, which Martens
began designing on 1990

OASE
35

Tijdschrift voor architectuur / Journal for Architecture

Stedelijke
formatie &
collectieve
ruimten

Urban
Formation &
Collective
Spaces

Tijdschrift voor architectuur   Het wereldontwerp /
Michiel Riedijk Het wereldontwerp / Erik Terlouw De grenzen van de tuin /
Robert-Jan van Pelt Mens en kosmos in Huygens' Hofwijck /
Pieter van Wesemael Mundaneum en Cité Mondiale /
Karel Teige Mundaneum / Le Corbusier Ter verdediging van de architectuur /
Richard Buckminster Fuller Het wereldspel – Hoe laten we de wereld werken /
Jurjen Zeinstra Het wereldbewustzijn van Richard Buckminster Fuller

OASE 41

UAS
Archit
& Lite
Bespiegeling /
verbeelding

ISBN 90-5662-487-3

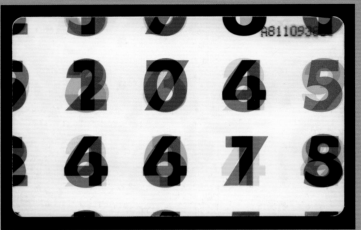

01 Two of Martens' designs
for standard telephone
cards, PTT Telecom/PTT
Kunst & Vormgeving, 1994

02 Wenspostzegels ('good-will'
stamps), for PTT Post/ PTT
Kunst & Vormgeving, 1997

Opposite: New year print, 2006,
monoprint, from an ongoing
series of uncommissioned work
and printing experiments,
1960—now

Martens had been given a brief by PTT to create a standard, everyday card design for seven denominations, so he joined up the dots between the client, the format, the audience and his own ever-present fascination for numbers and awe for colour to find a solution. "For me it is a miracle that I can press a number and another number in combination and get in touch with you or you—we take it all as normal. Another fascination for me is the nature of colour—that every reproduction can be made by the use of three primary colours—that's unbelievable in a way. So I put those things together…"

Each card features a pattern of numbers overprinted in different colours. They are not random, but based on a clever code where different combinations of colours and numbers represent a letter of the alphabet. On the cards this spells out the words of the Dutch national anthem. The project is an example of the beautiful way Martens synchronises logic and order with a sense of wonder and an emotive response to the world. He enjoys the beauty of mathematics, which is something he first encountered at school and has led to more recent explorations into how mathematics can formalise visual representation, such as the Arabic system of counting that is the basis for the intricate patterns and variations that are used as decoration in Arabic architecture.

The alphabet is another phenomenon for Martens, something that is reflected in the very type-oriented nature of his practice since the 1960s and the presence of a great many books and book cover designs in his oeuvre. "I see the alphabet as a miracle—twenty-six characters and you can make them do so many different things," he says. "There is no one page in all the books in the world that is the same—not even one line—that's unbelievably fascinating for me."

At the heart of Martens' studio, and perhaps at the heart of his current practice, is the workbench where he spends time making monoprints using found flat metal objects (discarded car parts, Meccano, mysterious discs, things he finds lying in the road) to print ink onto found paper. This 'free' practice (he seldom makes these prints to commission) distils Martens' way of working. Carefully, slowly, by hand—elongating the printing process to an almost meditative speed—he builds up a print from carefully chosen elements, printing one colour one day, waiting for it to dry and printing the next colour the following day. "Still I'm surprised that red and yellow becomes orange," he marvels.

"It's a kind of refuge," Martens continues about his monoprinting, "a garden for design, a try-out garden. And I'm my own boss when I am printing… it feels good to do it." When we visit, Martens is in the middle of printing the diplomas for students at Werkplaats—every student gets a handmade print by way of a certificate. He shows us the paper he's using to print them—salvaged archive papers from the Stedelijk Museum from the time Martens worked there one day a week with Wim Crouwel. The Stedelijk catalogues were in the process of being digitised and the old archive cards (which had been designed by Willem Sandberg during his time at the museum from 1945 to 1963) were being thrown out. Martens liberated them from the trash and has been using these unique documents as substrates for his prints ever since. Thus each print tells a fascinating design story, documenting not only the details of an artifact in the Stedelijk's collection but also embodying layers of Dutch design history, from Sandberg, through Crouwel and Martens, to the Werkplaats students who will receive it as their diploma.

"Design determines the quality of our common life," Martens wrote in Printed Matter, and it's clear that here is one designer who truly lives by such a mantra.

# Photography

Defining photography can be a knotty issue—is it all surface, or collections of printed objects, or just a screen-based amalgamation of noughts and ones? Photography's changing modes of execution, dissemination and consumption are addressed in our three special report articles this month. Jason Jules has pinpointed the moments where photography has defined masculinity in pop culture; James Langdon investigates how the edges of photographs frame the world; and Laura Clayton talks to Jason Evans about his subversive take on photography online.

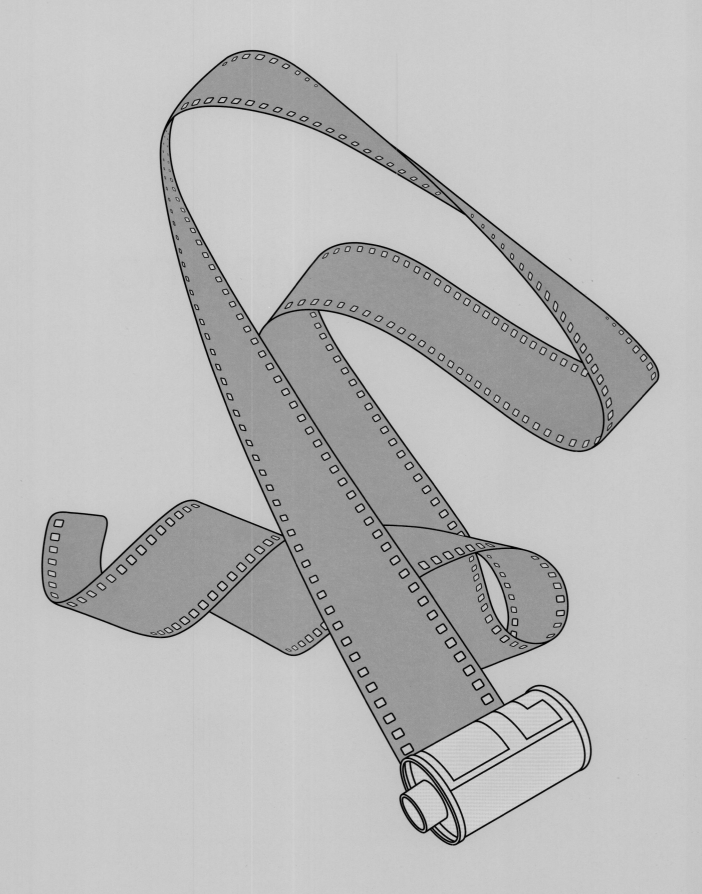

# Boys Keep Swinging

**An exploration of defining moments in the depiction of men in photography reveals an interesting twist in the portrayal of masculinity. As JASON JULES discovers, the old male stereotypes personified by the Village People can crystalise into lucid three dimensions in the hands of photographers and stylists who mainline the zeitgeist.**

What can you do? If you can't beat them, join them. And if you don't want to join them — subvert them. Some of the most memorable and impactful images of masculinity over the past forty or so years have come about through the work of the fashion photographers' and stylists' desires to confront and challenge the accepted definitions of what it means to be a man.

The stereotype images of masculinity that Village People play up to are not just gay-fantasies; they're very much part of a masculine image bank traditionally referenced by mainstream society as a whole.

The seminal images in the following pages often come out of an unspoken agreement between the stylist, photographer, magazine and model, whereby a weird chemistry takes received logic and turns it on its head. It's not just the clothing, the pose or the composition of the shot that creates a graphically arresting image; it's also a matter of timing. In terms of fashion photography the trends, ideas, politics and social concerns of the day provide the most significant frame for the work. After all, it is fashion photography we're talking about, not art... right?

# The Lawman

If villains and bad guys become celebrities and are afforded the same quality of attention as heroes and honourables, then where does that leave the good guys? This is one of the questions which David Bailey forced the viewer to explore when he fixed his lens on the notorious Kray brothers back in 1965.

By definition, fashion and style photographers have a keen sense of the directional, of the changing times and where they are heading. It's an ability to crystallise the moment yet to come. Here Bailey is not only playing with ideas of celebrity, referencing Warhol's "everyone will be famous for 15 minutes" quote, he is also questioning those long-established tenets of social hierarchy and authority — the police, the legal system and the class system all get challenged here. Picking up on a sensibility that a few years later would lead to the hippy movement and the student riots of '68, through fashion portraiture, Bailey replaces the Lord with the lowly and asks us to recognise the seeds of a forthcoming upheaval.

The Kray brothers, photograph by David Bailey, 1965

# The Leather Biker

By definition there's nothing pure about nostalgia. Nick Clements' work takes the viewer to a romanticised location, one that is visualised through the past but informed by concerns of the day. Here London-based photographer Clements can play with ideas surrounding the roles of men and women because we as the audience are already aware of what those roles are supposedly meant to be… or are we? Visually, by referencing archive photography, vintage props and authentic styling as well as character casting, Clements is also building on the work of the likes of Herb Ritts and Bruce Weber. In a sense Clements is not merely attempting to reclaim the stylistic territory of the leather-clad biker, but also affectionately gesturing towards gender values now seen by many as lost. As a piece of romance, his statement seems to long not for a forgotten age where male domination was key, but for the certainty and sense of glamour that were attached to that age.

Photography by Nick Clements for Intersection magazine issue 8, 2004

# The Construction Worker

Photograph by Kiyotaka Hatanaka, shoot for Tenderloin, Huge Magazine, issue 029, November 2006

This picture involves very current ideas surrounding the male image and the use of masculine iconography. Within it lie traces of all the other images mentioned here. It captures the stylistic interface between Britain, Japan and the mythical blue-collar American Hero — the construction worker. This is a fashion story featuring the Japan-based brand Tenderloin, whose clothing replicates vintage American workwear, often to a design spec and with an attention to detail way in excess of the original garments.

    The models are Britain-based men — real people as opposed to professional models. Just as it took years to acquire their tattoos, their style is not transient, it's part of a "long now", to use Eno's term. It harks back to ideas of masculinity from the Forties and Fifties and yet is very much part of today's street culture.

# The American Indian

Ray Petri is the godfather of modern styling. Working mainly with the Face, i-D and Arena, he was predicting and helping to shape a space where the likes of Simon Foxton, Edward Enninful, Karl Templer and Katie Grand could flourish. More than simply creating beautiful images, Petri was one of the first stylists to use the creative process of the fashion story to interrupt the usual reverie with which most men's fashion stories were consumed, by creating layers and contradictory narratives within a single story. He was articulating an aesthetic resistance to the conspicuous consumerism of the time.

This image is a case in point. Here Petri combines two conflicting ideas to create a tension between the powerful and the powerless. But not only is he challenging historical notions of power and identity, he's taking on a contemporary battle as well. In a time when the likes of photographer Bruce Weber and designers such as Ralph Lauren and Calvin Klein are presenting an idyllic WASP-like vision of the American Dream through their global advertising campaigns, Petri elegantly undermines these ideas. His proposition seems oppositional and yet complex; it's as if he's asserting that race, power, gender, and value — none of these cultural ideas is fixed. It's a liberating argument that runs through much of his great work, and still twenty years after his death provides a benchmark for the world of stylists today.

Photograph by Jamie Morgan, styled by Ray Petri, The Face, issue 10, 1985

**Special Report** Photography

# The Cowboy

Until recently Foxton has been one of menswear's best-kept secrets. Having worked with brands such as Fred Perry, Caterpillar, Levi's and Kilgore, he also helped launch the career of stylist Edward Enninful (Prada, Italian Vogue) and has been a great supporter of younger designers such as Carrie Mundane (aka Cassette Playa).

He worked with occasional collaborator and fellow i-D magazine alumnus Nick Knight on this seminal image, part of an ad campaign for Levi's. Here Foxton takes not just the standard ideal of the cowboy, but also our notion of what Levi's heritage means, and forces us to question both. The cowboy is the man's man, the mythical All-American. Along with Coca-Cola and rock 'n' roll, it has been one of America's greatest cultural exports.

One of the inconvenient elements of the Wild West narrative was — and still is — the roles played by black people at the time and how they fitted — or failure to fit — into Hollywood's fantasised story of the cowboy. Among black audiences, the standard joke was not IF, but WHEN the token black character was going to get killed off — as he always did — during the film.

In the UK especially, fed the Cowboy myth through years of Marlboro Man ads, the concept of the cowboy seemed to many to exist to affirm a sense of white male dominance within society.

Like Petri before him, Foxton takes received ideas of what it means to be a man and challenges them, using one of the most sacred icons in American culture to do so. This singular, arresting image highlights age, race, sexuality and historical authenticity. As glamorous as he looks, as stylised as he looks, this is not a fictional Hollywood creation. His name's Alonzo, he was 86 at the time and based in Colorado. He was also a real cowboy. Through i-D magazine, one of menswear's greatest tools has been street casting, using non-models in fashion-focused settings. Here Foxton, like Bailey and Petri before him, uses this tool to great effect.

Photograph by Nick Knight, styled by Simon Foxton, for Levi's

# The Military Man

It was a time when power cuts and mass redundancies, miners' strikes, car workers' strikes, dustbin men's strikes, and rows between the unions and the government provided the material for the tabloids and the broadsheets alike. By spring 1974 the death toll due to the Northern Ireland conflict had risen to 1,000 people. For the first time, wrestling was popular on TV, broadcast on Saturday afternoons.

Although at first glance it might seem unlikely, this image of Bryan Ferry from 1976 has everything to do with that period of time. Many would like to see it as part of Ferry's personal obsession with the surface, with image and style and part of a fashion culture, which included the likes of Biba, Ossie Clarke and Zandra Rhodes. Well, yes and no.

In a period where masculine prowess and men's struggle to dominate each other and anyone else who got in the way was evident in almost every element of public life, Ferry took the language of heroism and power and offered a new way of seeing masculinity. Ferry was one of the first to give a visual coding to post-modern cool – where aspiration and not brute force or strength was the key to success.

A working-class boy, born in Washington outside Durham, and an only child whose dad looked after pit ponies, Ferry recognised that the traditional male role models and social status quo required a degree of reassemblage. There he is, looking defiantly at the camera, part seducer, part seduced, informed and aware of the conflicts we all at some point face in our evolution, offering style as the perfect solution.

Bryan Ferry, photograph by Jorgen Angel, 1976, courtesy Getty/Redferns

# Everyday Niceties

## Everyday

## Everyday

Jason Evans is probably the only person on the planet who is baffled by the popularity of his online photography project The Daily Nice. LAURA CLAYTON toasts muffins and knocks back the jam with him (and a pop star friend) on a Sunday morning, and discovers that the smallest of pleasures make everything... nice.

## Everyday

## Everyday

## Everyday

Jason Evans wants to inject a little positivity. Every day, before he goes to bed, he selects one photograph from a folder of digital images he has taken, and uploads it to his website, The Daily Nice, where it remains for twenty-four hours. The next day, as if by magic, a new image appears, the previous one having disappeared into the ether. Just one page, one image, for one day, for free. It's as simple as that, and it's a ritual Evans has been carrying out for the last five years since he launched The Daily Nice in 2004.

Evans is a veteran fashion, music and documentary photographer who teaches at Farnham College of Art, curates exhibitions and contributes boundary-pushing articles to top photography journals, and I'm desperate to find out more about his past endeavours. However, he is about as reluctant to discuss his 'career' (and I use inverted commas, because the very mention of the word sends him into spasms of discomfort) as he is to limit himself to just one pursuit. Evans gives little away about his past successes (this a man who

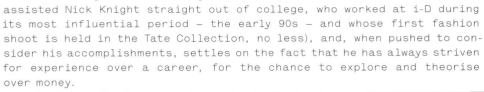

assisted Nick Knight straight out of college, who worked at i-D during its most influential period — the early 90s — and whose first fashion shoot is held in the Tate Collection, no less), and, when pushed to consider his accomplishments, settles on the fact that he has always striven for experience over a career, for the chance to explore and theorise over money.

In fact, finding anything out about the twenty years Evans has spent, camera in hand, creating work for the likes of Arena Homme Plus and Pop and Nick Knight's SHOWstudio, and producing countless record sleeves and work for Levi's, for example, is a treasure hunt in itself. The more you search, the more you find, and the more eclectic and impressive it gets. Even the fact that Evans brings along old friend Colin Greenwood of Radiohead (whom he's been teaching to take photos) to our Sunday brunch meet couldn't be more low-key. For a modern-day musical legend, Greenwood sits very patiently reading the Observer and drinking tea while we grapple with the role of photography in cyberspace.

The most hyped-up thing about the few hours Evans and I (and Greenwood) spend drinking coffee and toasting muffins is the venue itself: the jaw-droppingly décored, if not bizarrely named, Bob Bob Ricard in Soho. "I love it in here," enthuses Evans. "It's a bit overpriced and the food's so-so, but the interior is incredible, I have a thing about booths." And he's right. As we sit on Edwardian train carriage-inspired Peacock blue leather, complemented by gold metal accents and gargantuan Cubist light fittings, feeling far more glamorous than one ought to on a Sunday morning, I ponder Evans's specific artistic path. It's one that favours aesthetics over everything, the pleasure of discovering beauty in the mundane, and couldn't be more bloody genuine if it tried.

As you probably guessed, we're here to talk about The Daily Nice, which, bafflingly to Evans, is experiencing a surge in interest and popularity thanks to its refreshing take on how we consume photography on the internet. "It's basically my personal therapy project," concedes Evans, who has battled with mood swings since his teens. "I just find the media we're exposed to is so pessimistic and I think if you live your life looking for small pleasures, you'll find them and life becomes its own reward." Christened The Daily Nice as an antithesis to the renowned negativity of The Daily Mail, the site also plays with contemporary notions of photography consumption, utilising available and current technologies, as Evans explains: "I'm not a digital photographer but digital photography and the web give me this opportunity to create something that a lot of people can look at and it would be churlish not to engage with that."

In 2003, Evans received, quite out of the blue, the commission of a lifetime from Japanese cosmetics giant Shiseido, which set the framework for The Daily Nice. "They paid for me to go round the world for two months, anywhere I liked, and I had to photograph something that I thought was beautiful every day," says Evans. "Each day I sent my image and it was mounted and displayed in a gallery in Paris, which gradually filled up over the weeks, as well as on a website." The Beauty Where You Find It brief took him from Kenya. Chandigarh and Myanmar to the Australian Blue Mountains, New Zealand, Chile and Brasilia, and also offered a chance to finish up another diary-style personal series of interesting, out-of-context images, The New Scent, shot on black and white Ilford stock.

"It was pretty cool, but the problem was I did it by myself," reflects Evans. "I mean, I saw so many amazing things but an amazing thing is much more fun when it's shared; it also meant going to a lot of airports, and airports aren't fun. In New Zealand they had me in immigration for three hours as, thanks to my crazy itinerary, they assumed that I was a drug trafficker rather than artist."

So what makes a Daily Nice anyway? "It's a feeling. If I could put it into words, then I wouldn't have to take it," says Evans. "My students call me a magpie. I get intense pleasure from looking, especially if it's shiny or brightly coloured. I'm also a bit of a tree-hugger so I'm always out and about in nature. I seem to find more nices where the sun's out as sunshine makes all the colours bolder." Indeed, saturated colours and a graphic sense of composition are what typify a Daily Nice shot. Evans has a fascination with pattern, and so sequences of images with spots, stripes or similar colourways frequently occur. Animals also rate highly, as well as flowers. Each shot, however is always deliciously out of context, bereft of explanation and, sometimes, not even obviously 'nice'.

"I'm really excited by the ambiguity of photography," agrees Evans. "I like the fact that socially people think that photography is a way of recording and relaying information whereas in fact all photographs do is confuse reality. Unless a photograph has a context, it's totally open to interpretation, and the only context for The Daily Nice is that it's nice. I could photograph a shit, it could be a shit from my favourite dog, therefore it's a nice shit, but it's still a shit. So sometimes if I'm feeling a playful, I'll mess around with that."

Evans shoots all his nices, somewhat surprisingly, on a bog-standard Sony Cybershot digital camera, which he favours for its saturated colours and flash-to-lens proximity (for a great drop shadow). "I've always used funny little cameras. I'm not a camera snob, or a photography snob really," he explains. And the results are convincing; one look at a Daily Nice shot is enough to dispel any analogue-over-digital preciousness.

"It's useless being precious on the internet anyway because you have no control; everyone's monitor has a different calibration and if you're particularly excited by colour or contrast then what I'm seeing on my screen might be quite different to what you're seeing on your screen," grants Evans. "There is also a flattening that happens on the net where a drawing and a painting and a documentary photograph and a fashion photograph start to have the same surface and all the subtlety of production is stripped away from them. They stop being photographs and they become images, so you have to be pragmatic about it. That's why books and exhibitions are still important and will continue to be important."

Indeed, while Evans's previous diary project The New Scent is also currently living on the internet, its (anti-Cybershot) high-contrast, black and white analogue aesthetic has been treated to a book-like layout: complete with a table of contents, introduction and biography. It's a project that was originally envisioned as a book, and one that has since been exhibited. So do these images have a higher cultural worth than the Daily Nices? Why have two such contradictory web presences?

"That was my intention. I think the idea of having a style is irrelevant — I don't recognise my aesthetic, other people do," says Evans. "When you collaborate with as many people as I do, you begin to think, is that Simon Foxton's aesthetic or my aesthetic? I think I wear different hats when I'm working with different people and on different projects." So with its one-a-day throwaway format, how ought the Daily Nice to be consumed? "It's designed to be a homepage, but I can identify various kinds of user," reveals Evans. "There are those who look every morning, people who only look at it when they're unhappy, and then those who look at it for a month, get bored, then never come back."

As we run out of coffee, and anything left to toast, there's just one more thing I'm dying to know; does the pressure of pleasing his legions of followers ever get to Evans? Does he ever not feel like uploading something new? "I do get bored of my surroundings, particularly as I'm travelling far less now, but I tend to counteract that by not staying anywhere for more than three years," he says. And seeing as he's about to relocate from Farnham to Wales in order to begin teaching at Newport School of Art, there'll be no danger of The Daily Nice fizzling out any time soon. "There have been occasions where I've forgotten the charger for my laptop, or haven't been able to get internet access or whatever and I've not been able to change the site," says Evans. "People email me going, 'Are you ok? The Daily Nice hasn't changed for two days.' And I have to say, 'Sorry, I'm stuck in an airport.'"

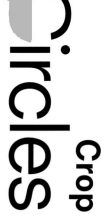

Crop
# Circles

Crop
Circles

Crop
Circles

Crop
Circles

**The default method of framing images in photography (not to mention graphic design) is between the four forty-five-degree angles and perpendicular edges of a rectangle. But, as JAMES LANGDON discovers, a more eccentric approach to framing and cropping can be found by tracing the evolution both of the photographic process and our way of seeing.**

My attention has recently been caught by a series of encounters with unusually cropped photographs. We generally understand the term 'cropping' as the practice of narrowing the rectangular frame of an image to remove anything that is not useful to the message being delivered. Or, in a more positive sense, precisely focusing on a specific subject. But its fullest meaning might also include the framing and editing of images in many forms: from the simplest of graphic devices — an oval frame, perhaps — to montage, collage and the dark arts of doctoring and retouching photographs. In post-revolutionary Russia, for example, having declared Trotsky an enemy of the people, the dictator Stalin had the image of his rival removed from numerous significant documentary photographs. This was undoubtedly an act of cropping.

In a history of images, cropping may be a recent phenomenon, certainly tied closely to the invention of photography and the emergence of mechanically mediated images. Today we find that the means by which photographic images have come to be recorded and distributed — film, sheet paper, digital sensor, computer screen — are almost always rectangular. And yet the rectangular frame is not essential to the production and reproduction of images. It is a construct: a convention that rationalises the display of images. The origins of this construct are in the methodologies of industrial production, but its impact on the way we read images should not be overlooked. The collection that follows here is by no means an exhaustive body of research, more a brief typology of images that share a healthy self-consciousness about their edges.

# John Baldessari Close-Cropped Tales

John Baldessari's book Close-Cropped Tales presents, in six parts, a series of found photographs cropped into polygonal frames of three, four, five, six, seven and eight sides. The photographs — most appearing to be production stills from action scenes in various obscure black-and-white Hollywood films — are a deadpan mixture of comic, slightly disturbing and puzzlingly ambiguous. The selection and cropping process is not arbitrary: it suggests a kind of reductive formal economy in which only the sites of specific narrative interest in an image are included in the frame. In one example from A Four-Sided Tale, a snake, a prostrate man and a barking dog occupy the three extremes of the frame, its constrained graphic form exaggerating the predicament of the subjects.

Each composition has an overt push-and-pull between what is included and excluded from view that functions contrary to the typically passive consumption of an image framed in a conventional rectangular format. Baldessari's angular cropping can only be read as reductive: we know that outside the frame exist portions of the image that the artist has chosen not to reveal. Simultaneously, the dynamic that these edgy graphic forms produce on the page has a disparity with their banal subject matter. The frames have an unfamiliar, clipped rhythm: their incongruity asserts the idea that the content of each image we encounter be considered directly and urgently in relation to its frame.

John Baldessari, from Close-Cropped Tales (CEPA Gallery, Buffalo, 1981)

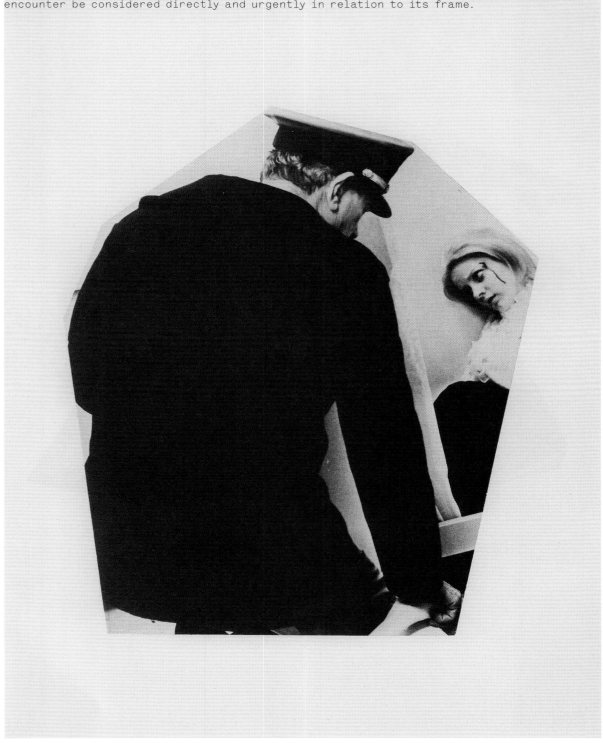

# Francis Bacon Incunabula

Often cropping and framing photographs is a process of straightening edges to make tidy graphic objects for a page layout. In exhibition catalogues, reproductions of paintings are routinely prepared with the corners and edges of their canvases cropped perfectly square, conforming to an expectation that paintings are primarily images rather than objects.

Yet cropping doesn't always mean narrowing or abbreviating. A beautiful example is a recent book documenting printed ephemera recovered from the artist Francis Bacon's studio after his death in 1992. Bacon hoarded great quantities of everyday printed matter in the studio: catalogues, magazines, newspapers and photographs, all of which were a source of reference in the process of painting. Over time these items would be folded or overpainted; sometimes incidentally, sometimes very deliberately emphasising or distorting particular imagery.

The treatment of this material in Martin Harrison's book seems to represent the fullest sense of what a reproduction can be: each item is scanned and digitally isolated with exceptional fidelity, and accompanied by comprehensive documentary provenance. The resulting images have an extraordinary quality on the page: the complexity of the unbound graphic forms produces a heightened sense of the presence of the original objects. Sometimes a single item will be shown in several arrangements, revealing the way in which its folding or marking might have been considered by Bacon. In the example here, a reproduction of a Rembrandt self-portrait has been repeatedly folded until the cracks in the paper's surface make distortions to the figure which are immediately suggestive of the distressed features of a Bacon portrait.

Ephemera as reproduced in Martin Harrison's Francis Bacon, Incunabula, Thames & Hudson, London, 2008

Sherrie Levine, President Collage #1, 1979. Collection Museum of Modern Art, New York. The Judith Rothschild Foundation Contemporary Drawings Collection Gift. Reproduced courtesy of Scala, Florence.

# Sherrie Levine President Collages

Some framing devices are commonly used to classify images. Think of a rounded rectangle identifying a still image from a television screen, or a light bulb appearing in a 'thought cloud' above a cartoon character's head as evidence of an idea dawning. Both of these examples are relatively neutral, in the sense that they are understood as aids to the clear expression of the context in which an image is intended to be read. A more coercive effect can be seen in numerous archetypal propaganda posters, where an ambient image of an agitated crowd or a symbolic piece of architecture might typically be framed inside the letterforms of a slogan.

American artist Sherrie Levine's series of President Collages use a framing device loaded in a more contrary spirit. Photographs of women from the pages of glossy magazines are cut out and framed by the graphic silhouettes of American Presidents, suggesting a commentary on the representation of gender and power. Despite this subversive shift, there is a clarity and directness in these compositions that could hardly be expressed more economically. Men are powerful, definitive and bold, their presence containing women, whose image is superficially glamorous or domestic. The frame here is more than a mute graphic form, it provides an active commentary on the image it holds.

# Joachim Schmid Photogenetic Draft

Counter to the idea of cropping loaded with a particular meaning might be a notion of arbitrary cropping. Yet this is a more problematic subject. How to remove or transgress the traces of meaning left by the action of cropping?

In 1990 German artist Joachim Schmid established the Institute for the Reprocessing of Used Photographs. This institutional alias disguised what was actually a one-man operation. Driven by a fascination with the global proliferation of photographic images, Schmid distributed through the press a polemical call to individuals and organisations requesting that they send their used photographic negatives for recycling at his 'facility'. Among many other materials (a collection which eventually consumed his Berlin apartment), the artist received a batch of negatives from a Bavarian firm specialising in individual studio portraits. Likely fearing that these might be used for some commercial gain, the sender had systematically cut each negative in half. In these spliced formats, Schmid discovered a kind of 'found' cropping, and began pairing fragments from different portraits with common proportions to produce what he calls Photogenetic Drafts.

The original action of cropping here is not an artful one, but a functional gesture of negation. In Schmid's recombinations that gesture is repurposed, becoming a restriction that is suggestive of new readings. Instead of limiting them, as was the intention, the cropped condition of these images extends their meaning beyond the original context of their production.

Joachim Schmid, Photogenetic Draft #24, 1990. Courtesy of the artist.

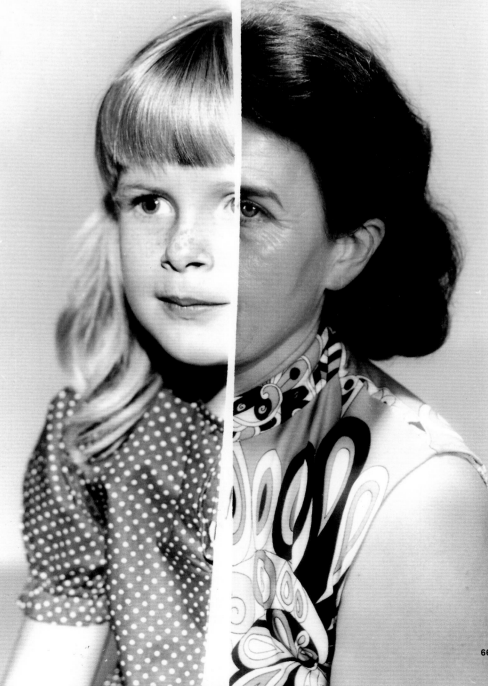

Jeff Wall, 8056 Beverly Blvd,
Los Angeles, 9am, 24 September, 1996.
Silver gelatin print, 203.5 x 256 cm.
Courtesy of Jeff Wall Studio.

# Jeff Wall 8056 Beverly Boulevard

"All lenses create circular images. Film is rectangular. Normally cameras are equipped with a lens that gives you an image bigger than the film being used, so the circular edges of the image are not recorded. When you use a bigger camera you have the option to change lenses, and change the relation between lens and film size. I like to do that sometimes because normally one never remembers that images are circular. Noticing it, experiencing it, tells you something about what photography really is, by means of reminding you about the relationship between the lens and the film." Jeff Wall

This image and the statement reproduced above reveal something of the prehistory of cropping and express succinctly the point of this enquiry: that making evident the mechanisms of cropping and framing refreshes our critical faculties and keeps us sensitive to what is happening at the edges of the images that we consume. Lastly, the idea expressed formally by this image in such a modest, matter-of-fact way extends the discussion here to include this most critical idea: that all images mediated by a lens are not inherently rectangular, and it naturally follows that they are almost all inherently cropped.

# 3 IS THE MAGIC NUMBER

**IT'S NOT FREE IT'S THREE**

Three copies of **grafik** for three pounds each.
Three pounds off every issue from then on!
Subscribe by direct debit and get your first three issues for £3 a copy.
And then pay just £18 per quarter (saving £3 on every issue).
*Apply using the form in Grafik, telephone +44 (0)1635 588 498
or subscribe online at grafikmagazine.co.uk
and use the code L10909 when prompted.
*This offer applies to UK residents with UK bank accounts only.

Free With Next Month's Grafik
## Letterform Collected
Out 17 September

112-page book featuring a compendium of Grafik's
Letterform articles August 2005 – August 2009,
along with newly commissioned work.

50 intriguing and inspiring letterforms
chosen and discussed by leading designers,
including Angus Hyland, Freda Sack,
Philippe Apeloig, Vince Frost, Daniel Eatock,
Henrik Kubel, Emmi Salonen, Jon Forss and more.

Letterform Collected is free to all UK and
international subscribers and UK bookshop
and newsstand customers.

# grafik¹⁷⁸

# Faces, one stop for everything font

:: Font licensing     :: Font consultancy

:: Custom fonts       :: Font asset management solutions

You'll find thousands of font products, from scores of foundries, on our website.

# www.faces.co.uk

## Click now to find, try, buy, download.

Competitive prices :: Special offers :: New releases :: Telephone support :: Online credit account

**01276 38888**   **info@faces.co.uk**

349 Yorktown Road, College Town, Sandhurst, Berks GU47 0PX

Copy set in Neo Tech, available from www.faces.co.uk. Online credit account subject to status. E&OE

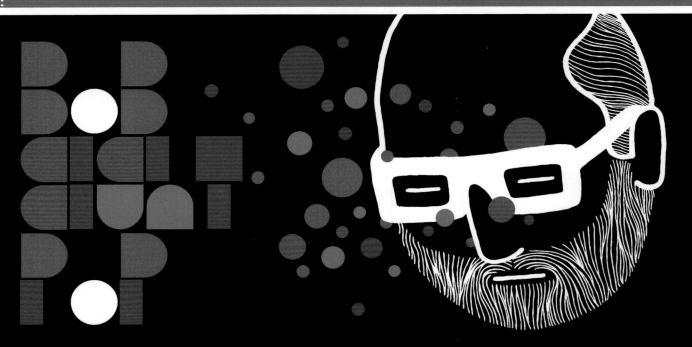

We are an award winning hand bench screen printing studio with over 25 years of experience producing beautifully executed print using specialist materials, finishes and processes - printing the unusual on to the unusual.

Call Bob or Liz to discuss your ideas: **0208 988 3335**          **www.bobeightpop.com**

View

# How to Be Green

**Powering computer equipment, travelling to the studio and meetings, disposing of waste, buying materials, motivating your team... With a little bit of creative thought and some excellent advice from NAT HUNTER, all these aspects of day-to-day work can be adapted to make you greener. Read on to find out how. Illustration by RICHARD HOGG.**

In an economic downturn businesses review every aspect of how they work, and it often turns out that much of a company's spending is inefficient or superfluous—only when the purse strings require tightening do we figure that out. Reassessing your business's environmental impact is similar—you'll wonder why you hadn't done it before. A long, hard look at your environmental impact will reveal ineffective and unproductive use of your resources that is easy to put right. And not only will you be helping to combat climate change, you should save yourself some cash.

Whether you have a studio of 100 people or it's just you at home with the cat, the same principles apply to an environmental review. One of the best ways to conduct a studio review is to get an objective outsider in for an analysis. Airside worked with an environmental certification auditor called Green Mark, which came in and went through everything we did and produced.

Their recommendations meant the introduction of numerous new initiatives and sometimes a complete overhaul of ingrained ways of working. They were the cause of frequent swearing from our studio manager, but by the end of the process the benefits were apparent and she had learned a lot. Plus we got a Green Mark certification, which is handy to mention when establishing environmental credentials with prospective clients.

Of course, it might not be necessary to call in the experts. Common sense and a tiny bit of technical knowledge go a long way. If you have someone in your organisation with the enthusiasm and interest to put in the time and effort, you can use the techniques we discussed in Grafik 175 to initiate a self-review. To get you started, here are five main areas to concentrate on.

**Waste:** A good waste minimisation system could save you up to one per cent of your turnover, so even a small studio with an annual turnover of £100,000 could save £1,000 a year. Start by thinking about everything you throw out and whether it has actually reached the end of its usefulness. Could you reuse the blank side of scrap paper to print that proposal you want to review on the train home? Why not reuse the padded envelopes you receive in the mail? You should find visits to the stationers becoming less frequent.

In most places it will cost more to send a kilo of rubbish to landfill than it will to recycle your waste. So reduce the amount that goes in your normal rubbish collection. Start by making everyone aware what can be recycled and then encourage them to consider every item they dispose of. One interesting idea is to remove individual wastebaskets from people's desks and have a central rubbish area, so people don't just toss things in the bin without thinking about it. Your recycling collector might only take the usual paper, plastic and glass, but a bit of research should help you find places that will take other stuff—CDs, ink cartridges, electronic items, batteries and food waste can all be recycled.

**Energy:** In this case "how can we save money?" and "how can we save the planet?" are the same question. The simple answer is a switch-off campaign to ensure that all lights, monitors, computers and other electrical equipment are turned off when not in use, especially overnight. Getting an energy monitor like Wattson or Owl is useful to give a tangible indicator of how many watts and how much money you are burning. Since Airside got one for Christmas, everyone has been trying to get the readings as low as possible. At the end of the day you find people wandering around the building switching things off.

You can also ensure your energy comes from a renewable source. Simply contact a company like Good Energy or Ecotricity and they'll handle the switchover for you. At the moment they might be slightly more expensive than your regular supplier, but as their customer base increases so their costs should come down.

**Transport:** Cars—much as we love them—are bad, especially when you have so many other options. Do people in your studio drive to work when there are buses and trains that could take them? You could even go on two wheels and buy a bike under the tax-break scheme offered by Cycle To Work.

Transport also has a less direct impact in terms of the things you buy. Just because you're not doing the driving doesn't mean it is nothing to do with you. Airside used to have big plastic bottles of filtered water delivered every week—until we installed a water filter on our taps, reducing costs, plastic use and our carbon emissions. It might be cheaper to get that flyer printed in Italy rather than the printers down the road, but if it is being flown in there's a hidden environmental cost.

**Purchasing and Procurement:** If you're reviewing your costs you'll need to spend some time analysing all your bills and receipts to see where the money goes. When you do this, you should also think about the environmental impact of each purchase. Where did it come from? Who made it? How is it made? Do this for everything, from biscuits to tea, pens to paper, couriers to taxis, printers to stationers, heat to light. Refer to our pen analogy from Grafik 175—can you apply this anywhere else?

**Awareness and Communication:** You can't do all of this alone (unless, of course, it is just you and the cat) so it's important to get everyone's interest and input from the start. It's useful to have an environmental policy which can act as a green mission statement and something to aim for. It's also a good thing for prospective clients to see on your website. These days, big companies have to at least pretend to be interested in the environment, so they'll need to know if you are before they can work with you.

These are just some of the ways in which you can attempt to change the habits of a lifetime. It's not always easy, it's not always cheap but it always makes the most sense. Once you've kicked the old routine you'll look back and laugh disbelievingly at how you used to do things, like a grown man seeing pictures of his awkward, long-haired teenage self. "Remember how we used to leave the computers on all night? Man, what were we thinking?"

LINKS FOR FURTHER READING:
    Green Mark: www.green-mark.co.uk
    Envirowise: www.envirowise.gov.uk
    Global Action Plan: www.globalactionplan.org.uk
    First Mile: www.thefirstmile.co.uk
    Ecotricity: www.ecotricity.co.uk
    Good Energy: www.goodenergy.co.uk
    Wattson: www.diykyoto.com/uk
    Owl: www.theowl.com
    Green Tomato cars: www.greentomatocars.com

The first time I looked at the V&A logo up close and was struck by its versatility was in 2001. I had won the pitch to design a 'temporary' website for the Victoria and Albert Museum. As part of this project I had to join the web development team 'inside' the museum walls once a week, which turned out to be a real treat. It felt a bit like working in the servants' quarters of Buckingham Palace. What a brilliant place, packed with extraordinary people.

The main attributes of the logo are elegance, simplicity and longevity. Just like the way the V&A's collection never ceases to find new audiences so the logo has stood the test of time. I just love this clever little twist of linking the ampersand and the A—a 'stroke' of genius there from Alan Fletcher.

I believe he designed it in 1989. The logo seems to be doing all the corporate work, as I can't really make out any other elements of the museum's corporate identity. A few years back, someone seems to have made a decision always to use the logo really prominently on all printed matter, and oddly it is always bleeding off the page too. I am not sure whether these 'rules' are not more of an obstacle than an inspiration for the design of the individual project. But the logo always seems to come out on top. It is more robust than expected from a word mark with such fragile Bodoni serifs.

I don't know what came first, the 'nickname' V&A or Alan's logo. Both continuously help to make the museum stay contemporary and accessible.

THE GOLDEN AGE
OF COUTURE:
PARIS AND LONDON
1947–1957
22 SEPTEMBER 2007–
20 JANUARY 2008
WWW.VAM.AC.UK

25 September 2008–
11 January 2009

John French,
Fashion Photograph,
1960s
©V&A Images

1947 © ASSOCIATION WILLY MAYWALD/ADAGP, PARIS AND DAKS, LONDON 2007

Replica uppercase 'R'
by NICOLE JACEK, KarlssonWilker

I have to apologise. I know neither of a typeface with hidden or unpublished characters, nor any other weird stories behind a font. Instead, I would like to showcase Replica—one of the most beautiful and smartest typefaces in recent years, which I have used for a book project for MoMA.

It was released in 2008 by our dear friends and heroes, designers Dimitri Bruni and Manuel Krebs of Norm. Manuel and Dimitri tried to create a neutral typeface, as timeless as possible, taking up the linear roman typefaces of the 1950s and 1960s. A pessimist would say that timelessness is impossible to achieve, but it can never hurt trying. (I myself never use Helvetica, which I assume is a typeface known for being 'timeless'.) Replica looks familiar from a distance, while from up close one can see the richness in details and variation. Replica obviously hints towards 'to replicate', an interesting point in this context. It also contains the French word 'réplique'. So Replica is a response to… what? Could it be Helvetica, since both end in '-ica'?

Let me go back to its design process: as the designers describe it, a "70" grid was used—

an anachronistic decision, since the trend is towards smaller and smaller grids. 700 units is the standard caps height in FontLab, meaning Dimitri and Manuel simplified it by a factor of 10, being aware of having fewer options and possibilities to place their nodes and Bezier control points. The second formal decision made was to cut off all corners, so that there are no right angles (which gives Replica its unique characteristic), along with a third decision, to cut diagonals. There are no pointed ends as might most likely be found on 'A', 'K' and 'R', so Replica letters can be set very closely. These striking bevels are clearly one of the main identifying features of the typeface (and the reason for my strong emotional reaction towards it). Replica comes as a small and exclusive font family (book, italic, bold, bold italic)—again—as simple as its design. Too much choice limits our lives. Long live Replica.

www.karlssonwilker.com
www.nicolejacek.com
www.norm.to

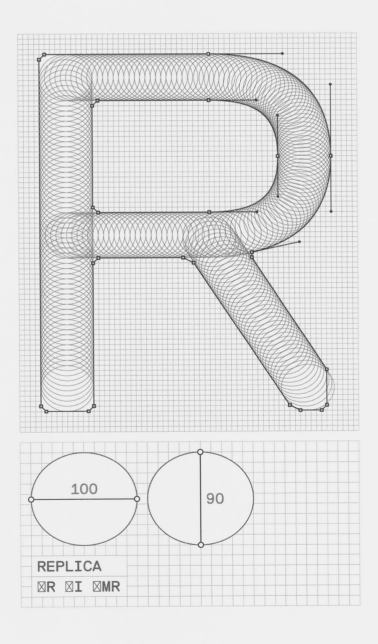

Extract from Replica specimen, showing vertical and horizontal stems/gauge balls, 2008

You could count on one hand the people who have truly changed the way we wear clothes in the last century. In his column this month HUGO dips into a small but very carefully chosen section of his bookshelf to introduce us to one of those characters. We give you Mademoiselle…

THE ALLURE OF CHANEL

the river; sand, white railings and, in the background, the hills of the Bourbonnais. The sun glinted on the slopes of Ganat. The jockeys and the stable lads followed one another, at a walk, their knees tucked under their chins.

"What a wonderful life," I sighed.

"It's mine all the year round," said M B. "I live in Com-piègne. Why shouldn't it be yours too?"

I said yes. I would never see Mont-Dore again. I would never see my aunts again.

That is my childhood, the childhood of an orphan, retold by a girl who knew no home, no love, no father and mother. It was terrible, but I don't regret a thing. I have been ungrateful to the wicked aunts: I owe them everything, a rebellious child makes for a well-prepared and very strong human being. (Aged eleven, I had much more strength than I do now.) It is kisses, hugs, teachers and vitamins that kill children ... prepare them for being weak or unhappy. It is wicked ... who make conquerors of them … And who develop ... rity complexes in them. In my case, this gave me the ... te: superiority complexes. Beneath maliciousness, ... strength; beneath pride, there is the taste for success ... love of importance. Children who have teachers ... as self-taught; I learnt badly, haphazardly. And yet, ... ut me in touch with those who were the most ... r brilliant people of my age, a Stravinsky, or a ... ther felt stupid, nor embarrassed. Why? ... ad worked out on my own that which cannot ... ll return to this frequently. For the time being, ... a this important aphorism, which is the secret

30

FROM COMPIÈGNE TO PAU

of my success, and perhaps that of civilisation; confronted with ruthless techniques of doing things: *it's with what cannot be taught that one succeeds.*

I had run away. My grandfather believed I had returned home; my aunts thought I was at my grandfather's house. Someone would eventually realise that I was neither with the one nor the other.

I had followed M B and I was living in Compiègne. I was very bored. I was constantly weeping. I had told him a whole litany of lies about my miserable childhood. I had to disabuse him. I wept for an entire year. The only happy times were those I spent on horseback, in the forest. I learnt to ride, for up until then I hadn't the first idea about riding horses. I was never a horsewoman, but at that time I couldn't even ride side-saddle … The fairy tale was over. I was nothing but a lost child. I didn't dare write to anyone. M B was frightened of the police. I didn't ... friends told him: "Coco is too young, send her back home." M B would have been delighted to see me go, but I had no home any more. M B had just broken off his relationship with a well-known beauty of the period, Émilienne d'Alençon; his house was full of photographs of her. "How lovely she is!" I said to him naively. "Could I meet her?" He shrugged his shoulders and replied that it was impossible. I didn't understand. M B was afraid of the police, and I was afraid of the servants. I had lied to M B. I had kept my age a secret, telling him that I was nearly twenty: in actual fact I was sixteen. I made an appearance at the Compiègne races. I wore a straw boater, set very low on the head, and a little country suit, and I followed events from the end of my lorgnette. I was convinced no one

31

The Allure of Chanel
By PAUL MORAND

Published by
Pushkin Press

£12.00

In my personal library, I try to have a lot on some subjects and a little bit on most everything else. A degree of depth and a degree of range. Fashion books are in the latter categories of 'a little bit' and 'range'. I'm slightly prejudiced against them generally, largely because there is so much tat floating in the book stream that it infects the whole of the published body. There is, however, a respectable body of book work to do with coffee-table fashion photography, especially concerning historical references. And every now and then something comes along or pops back up in fashion literature that really warrants a look. Our pages today come from such a work.

It relates the story of a young girl, having lived two lives already, lying about her age and jumping into a third. She literally walks away, never to return. In these two pages we get a perfect distillation of the cunning, insight and bravery that would mark out her life. In the page following the two you can see opposite, she leaves the new life she has only just described to go on to yet another, again, by simply walking away. The woman could be opportunistic and destructive. She took chances. Not all of them turned out for the better, but she survived and prospered. She had many more lives after these, some brilliant, not all of them wise, but she became someone: Coco Chanel. Or, as we know her today post-mortem, Chanel. Having read this book, you will see why hers is the greatest name in fashion.

The book is The Allure of Chanel, by Paul Morand, published as seen here by the quietly wonderful Pushkin Press. It is, without doubt, one of the greatest books of fashion memoir ever written. And it is one of the better 'celebrity' life memoirs ever put to page as well. Paul Morand met a washed-up Chanel in St Moritz in 1946 with a view to writing her memoirs. The memoirs never happened. The notes he had written of their conversations were put away in a drawer, forgotten, and only resurfaced by chance after Chanel's death in 1971. It is from these notes that Mr Morand wrote this book, essentially a written record of a very long and revelatory conversation. Or, more likely, notes from a monologue.

In last month's column, we looked at Henry James, one of the latter and better upholders of Victorian decency, stuffiness and ridiculousness. With Coco Chanel, "the exterminating angel of nineteenth-century style", we find someone who helped move life far away from that old world and into the 'new' world after the Second World War. Her revolution concerned not only women's clothing, but also attitudes and lifestyle. Chanel hated profoundly the layered and corseted dress of the nineteenth century. You can understand why when you read her views on the subject, having grown up in the old world's autumn. She saw it for what it was: with 'respectable' and 'reverential' veneers,

the nineteenth-century lady, always on a plinth, was in fact Chinese foot-bound all the way to the top of her head, a living mummification of a woman's body, hiding natural form, inhibiting natural joy, and restricting movement in time and place and, by extension, mind. With this 'dress' came in tow all the enforced stupidity and unavoidable laziness of up-market indentured servitude: they dressed that way because they lived that way, they lived that way because they dressed that way. The subjugation of women had reached a fitting apogee in the 'costume' (for that is what is was; it certainly was not 'clothes') of the pre-First World War lady. And if 'lady' meant virtually all of the women from the middle classes on up, and many others aspiring to be there, that was a vast number of women.

But here comes this crazed, lonely, orphaned peasant girl, raised by wicked witches and somehow coming through it with the one attribute needed to revolutionise the dressed world of women: a superiority complex. She learned to learn as life showed her, with few teachers, and many mistakes and awkward moments, her mind a stitched mix of sublime dreams and very hard realities. Like a thin wet cat, angry and looking for warmth, she twisted and scratched ever upwards to get what and where she desired. She got there. She used cunning, charm and a keen intelligence, laced with very hard work. She fought weaknesses in herself relentlessly, and those weaknesses that she could not slay, she pimped; she was certainly not going to be defeated by any army within herself when she had so many to do battle with around her. She had scores to settle with the world, and she settled them. Some of them, like freeing women from the bondage of nineteenth-century fashion, were of the highest social importance and good. She was a significant part of that time's massive change in social relations between classes and occupations, largely because she was obsessed with quality, style and utility, and it mattered not from where they came. Other scores were often petty, arbitrary and vindictive, but in this respect she could remind one of Lord Nelson, "Never explain, never apologise, and never look back." She did not. She was horny, famous and rich. She was hard, clear and phenomenally good.

Once, in the bloom of her youth, she fell truly, madly and deeply in love. But only once. The boy died in a motor accident, and she speaks little of losing him in this book. It still hurt too much in 1946, decades after she lost him. Thereafter she loved only work, her work, but any kind of career with worldly success would have done. She knew herself: achievement, riches and destiny. She had earned these things. She paid for these things with a deep personal loneliness, but for Mademoiselle there was no other consideration. Having truly loved once, thereafter her allure was hers alone. And ours too, for a price.

# Viewpoint

**Which is your photograph that got away?**

## SARA SHAMSAVARI

As an artist and street photographer much of my interest lies within bridging the gap between high art and the community. In 2007 I was at an artists' talk at the Powerhouse Arena in Dumbo, Brooklyn. There was a show on of the work of Jamel Shabazz and Leonard Freed. While the artist talks were going on two workers in heavy blue and fluorescent yellow overalls walked into the gallery and stayed to appreciate the art on the walls. Out of respect for the artists speaking I did not get the shot out of fear that I would disrupt the environment. Later on when I told Shabazz, he assured me the opportunity would come around again and said, "Always be ready."

www.sarashamsavari.com

## RALF OBERGFELL

During the last World Cup I was working on a self-assigned street life project. The kids would dress up in Union Jacks and watch the games.

Shooting was going well but it all began to feel strange when the image counter on the SLR wouldn't stop after thirty-six frames. When I rewound the film I realised it wasn't loaded. My jaw dropped, I felt some anger and sadness, because the shoot captured many 'images of the moment' that were impossible to re-create.

Looking at it now, I may still be a little sad about that special lost body of work, but I can also laugh about it. I think it was one of those moments that may have happened to many, if not all, photographers at some point in their careers.

www.ralfobergfell.com

## ASLAK GURHOLT RØNSEN, YOKOLAND

One day about two yeas ago I looked out the window of our studio and saw that the only cars parked outside were five red ones parked in a row. An amazing coincidence that needed preserving; I dashed out to take a picture. Unfortunately what I didn't realise was that there was a drug deal going on in one of the cars. They weren't too happy to be included in the picture and I decided that the best thing to do was to make an exit before I had to explain further.

www.yokoland.com

## KIM HOLTERMAND

I had spotted some greenhouses from the motorway which glowed in the sky at night, almost like a surreal scene from an episode of X-Files. I contacted the person in charge and arranged to shoot them at night, making sure that they would keep the light on for the evening. However, when I reached the greenhouses on the night of the shoot, the whole building was blacked out. I have tried to shoot the greenhouses several times since and every time I get there they're not glowing at all. It's one of those shoots that I will keep trying to do and hopefully some day I will succeed.

www.holtermand.dk

## PAUL FARRINGTON, STUDIO TONNE

Photography for me has always been about luck; my best photographs have always been taken with either a Lomo or a Polaroid.

Before computers, I used to do all my image work on a photomechanical transfer camera. It was great, as it allowed for random things to happen in the way an image could be processed; the dirtier the chemicals, the better the image was my trick.

In my own work I don't really use photography and prefer to create illustrations, but what I do use is when the computer freezes and the screen goes all weird and pixellated I take a screenshot. It works sometimes even though the laptop restarts and I can lose the shot.

www.studiotonne.com

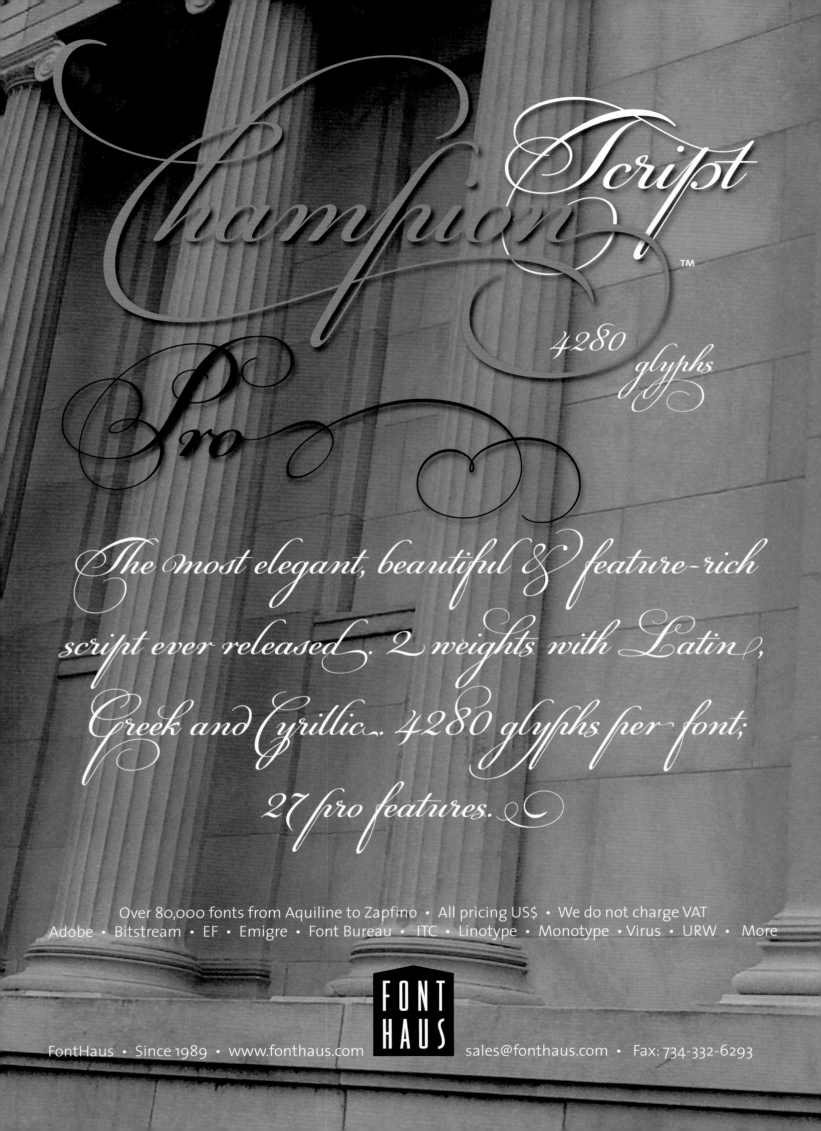

*Champion Script Pro*

4280 glyphs

*The most elegant, beautiful & feature-rich script ever released. 2 weights with Latin, Greek and Cyrillic. 4280 glyphs per font; 27 pro features.*

# *Mustard*

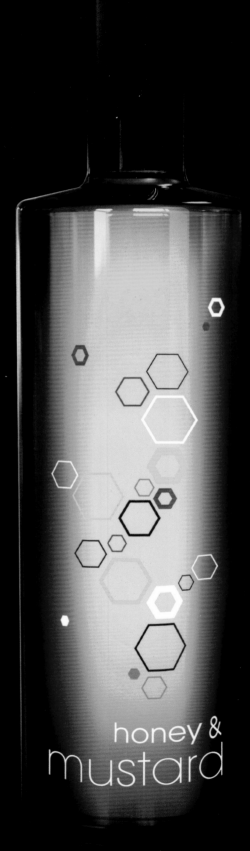

It's a little unsung, the power of partnership in recruitment. Try pouring honey all over your lettuce with not a lot else, and see how it goes down. Some things just work well in tandem, and go places together they simply can't alone. So to really make your salad sing, ally your sweet charms with something that really knows how to complement them.

Www.wearemustard.com

**Recruiting for the industry leaders.**

Say hello on 020 7357 9333 or email
hello@wearemustard.com
Mustard, First Floor, 57a Lant Street
Borough, London SE1 1QN

honey &
mustard

# Review

**Modell Bauhaus**
Martin-Gropius-Bau,
Berlin,
Until 4 October 2009
Reviewed by
ANTHONY NOEL

Forged between the two World Wars in one of history's regular lows, the modernist project, as epitomised by the Bauhaus, left us a highly visible record of its failures. So much so that it is hard to look past the oxidised concrete façades of the housing schemes and the soulless machines for living that were the eventual outcome of one of the greatest, most unified creative efforts by the design disciplines to improve the human condition. Now that we've apparently returned to another of history's dips, maybe it is part serendipity, and part of this cycle of history, that a major new collaborative exhibition by Germany's three Bauhaus institutions is opening now. In some ways it is simply a tectonically slow political process that has meant it has taken this long since the fall of the Wall for Germany's three Bauhaus institutions — the Bauhaus University Weimar, Stiftung Bauhaus Dessau and Bauhaus Archive Berlin — to come together for the first time and create this show, the largest exhibition on the Bauhaus yet.

Focusing on the short history of the design school, its founding context and politically motivated dissolution, the show departs from the principles of earlier exhibitions in that it is not built around the output of the various workshops, but rather progresses in a chronological order; true to the multi-disciplinary ethos of the school, architectural projects are displayed alongside products, graphic and typography designs, free artistic practice, interiors and theatre sets.

I like the idea that this show, in a small way, is closure for the revolutionary, tumultuous world events at the start of the last century. It is a neat, theoretical contrivance, and anniversaries being the convenient conceptual peg that they are, it is a shame that I can't hang this notion off a centenary exhibition, but there's something in the fact that it took the worst humanitarian disaster in history to bring about the economic conditions that led to the foundation of the greatest optimistic, co-operative creative humanitarian effort; and that just a short fourteen years later, political forces with a distinctly regressive, anti-humanist agenda would, through repression and political pressure, force the Bauhaus's closure, leading to modernism's eventual dissemination throughout the world.

Walter Gropius, 1928 in front
of his design for the Chicago
Tribune Tower of 1922.
Photo: Associated Press,
Berlin Bauhaus-Archiv Berlin

MEISTER DOPPELHÄUSER von unten gesehen. 1926. ARNDT

That the modernist ideal became the motivation for the post-industrial and post-colonial move towards corporate globalisation would not have disturbed Walter Gropius, the Bauhaus's founder and first director. The gap between ideal and reality, between theory and praxis, is where individuals learn about their own abilities and limitations, the difference between talent and application, expectation and realisation. The modernist project may have fallen short of the aims set out by Gropius and his peers, but that doesn't negate the optimism behind the attempt.

So a big statement then? Is the show actually inviting a reappraisal of modernism? Probably not, and a good thing too. Instead, it sets its stall out as being nothing more than a long-awaited collaboration between the three holders of the flame, long separated by a Germany divided by the war that resulted from that same regressive, anti-humanist agenda, and leaves us to draw our own ideas and conclusions. But I am reminded of the fact that the modernist project wasn't simply dry, spiritless functionality. Set out across eighteen galleries in the Martin-Gropius-Bau, an Empire-era museum and exhibition hall built by a great uncle of Walter Gropius, and itself the victim of one World War, now restored and at the heart of Berlin's cultural landscape, each room has a focus, usually one of the masters or a historic event such as the World Fair, placing the artefacts on show in some kind of context. I found the detail on some of the political forces at play a little light; the firing of Hannes Meyer as school director, for example, and the school's two enforced moves are described as events, without much examination of the political motivations that led to their happening, aside from the implication that the Bauhaus's philosophy was at odds with the prevailing political climate. In this way the story of the Bauhaus's dissolution and subsequent dissemination feels a touch subjective, history as told by the — eventual — winner. But that is natural enough, and it is a beautiful point well made. Had the Nazis not suppressed the school and its neo-liberalist, elitist (in their eyes), progressive ideology, then its key proponents would not have felt compelled to flee the country and propagate their ideas and methods in more fertile and receptive soil. This repression in effect created a Bauhaus diaspora, particularly in the States where the founding masters were able at last to find the private patrons for their educational method that the German state had failed to provide.

Alfred Arndt, colour plans for the exterior design of the Bauhaus Masters' houses in Dessau, 1926. Bauhaus-Archiv Berlin © VG Bild-Kunst, Bonn 2009

This show is a big event in Berlin's summer programme, and will clearly be a major draw for visitors and Berliners alike. Look out for the entrance gate inspired by Kandinsky's Circle Triangle Square. The planning and sequencing are coherent and logical, tied together well by the scenography of Chezweitz & Roseapple, although I wasn't the only person who struggled to find the correct starting point, instead making a beeline for the central court which contained an interactive trade-show-style display inviting visitors to create their own Bauhaus. Mies van der Rohe's World Fair pavilion this wasn't, seemingly sponsored by Ikea and the museum gift shop, but it was a comfortable place to sit and draw a plan for my ideal apartment. Lining the walls facing into the courtyard is a historical, cultural and political timeline providing context for the displays in the galleries. Unfortunately, you don't realise it is there until you've been right through the galleries, so it feels like a bit of an afterthought and not as integral to the main narrative as it could have been. As it is, there's plenty to take in and the emphasis is rightly on the combined contributions of the three institutions (plus a few from MoMA New York) with just enough backstory to make you want buy the hefty 376-page catalogue for some quality loo-time reading.

**Chevolution**
ICA Films
Opens 18
September
Reviewed by
SCOTT KING

The most exciting aspects of Chevolution are the constant, but largely unexplored, contradictions at the heart of the story. As everybody knows Alberto Korda's famous image of the anti-capitalist revolutionary Che Guevara ("Guerrillero Heroico") has been appropriated by capitalism to sell everything from vodka to cigarettes to perfume. Not to mention, of course, millions of T-shirts, posters, badges... and even a few thongs.

The contradictions run deep: Ernesto 'Che' Guevara was a medical doctor turned armed revolutionary and "brutal assassin." Alberto Korda was a high-living fashion photographer (pre-revolution) turned photojournalist for the state-run newspaper Revolución. The Italian Giangiacomo Feltrinelli was a millionaire anarchist who produced the first few hundred thousand Che (as you know him) posters in order to solidify and perpetuate the anti-capitalist struggle: but succeeded largely in spawning a business model that someone in the 1980s would copy and rename Athena. Sadly, the film only skims over Giangiacomo Feltrinelli's involvement: sadly, because in many ways Feltrinelli's mass distribution of the Che image in poster form is the real thrust of the story.

As a film, Chevolution at first seems to be very linear — indeed, it starts at the beginning of Che Guevara's story, but it finishes in a circular manner somewhere near the middle of Guerrillero Heroico's story. It recounts Che's famous training as a doctor, Che's famous motorcycle journey to Mexico, Che's famous meeting with Fidel, but most of this we've seen before as documentary or cinema. There are some potentially great insights; an interview with Alberto Granado, Che's childhood friend, but even he describes Che as "superhuman", so we don't really become any wiser about the man behind the screenprint.

I hesitate to say Chevolution is a failure, because it isn't. Its problem is that it skims across such a huge story and so many issues that you're left thinking, "I could have worked that out for myself if I'd sat down and thought about it."

Che was not born Che, of course; he was born Ernesto. He became "Che" and consequently "CHE!" He invented himself with the help of the media — not dissimilar, in this sense, to Billy Fury, Alvin Stardust or Johnny Rotten — he had a made-up name that allowed him to become someone else, it allowed him to become an image — an idea. More than one interviewee picks up on this and, to be fair, the film makes clear that the image is almost an empty vessel that the viewer can project their own ideas of revolutionary righteousness onto, as illustrated here by citing the students of Paris '68, the Black Panthers and, erm, Rage Against the Machine.

The most insightful interviewee is Ivan de la Nuez who, from a darkened gothic room, tell us "capitalism destroys everything". Unfortunately, before he's allowed to expand on this he's cut short in favour of a teenage gork's view that Che was a symbol of "Totalitarian Socialism" (well, maybe, but it's hard to say as Che didn't hang around long enough to implement anything resembling a 'Total Totalitarianism'). Moments later an air-headed Republican student explains how her Che T-shirt is different from most people's because it bears the legend "Brought To You By Capitalism" under the Che graphic — she's clearly the type who enjoys wearing her T-shirt at the student bar, possibly in the hope of inciting punch in the braces in order to prove how evil Communism really is.

So. The problem with this film is that it tries to cover too much ground and consequently skims across the ultimate point: capitalism will disarm appropriate and resell absolutely anything in order to continue to refuel itself. That said, I dare say that one hundred hours of documentary footage still wouldn't get to the bottom of the inherent contradiction of the world's most famous revolutionary being used to sell cotton T-shirts that are manufactured in Indonesian sweatshops then sold to American tourists on Oxford Street by a Polish lad working weekends.

One line sticks in the mind — confronted by his assassin, Che is reported to have said, "Aim well. You are going to kill a man." These words could equally have been whispered in Alberto Korda's ear on March 1960 when he aimed his camera at Che Guevara and laid the foundation stone for a multimillion dollar myth industry.

uerrillero Heroico,
y Alberto Korda © 1960,
ourtesy Diana Diaz,
orda estate.

Six Books

Edited by
Cees W. de Jong,
Alston W. Purvis,
Jan Tholenaar

Type
A Visual
History
Typef
and
Gr
St

MICHAEL D

ABC OF MEN'S FASHION

**Beuys Is Here**
Published by De La
Warr Pavilion, £5.00

**ABC of Men's
Fashion**
By Hardy Amies
Published by
V&A, £9.99

**Beuys Is Here**

**Michael Doster
80s/90s**
Published by
Damiani, £45

dding to the already considerable back catalogue of
ooks on offer about the artist Joseph Beuys, this
ittle paperback (designed by the formidable talents
t Fraser Muggeridge Studio) manages to offer some-
hing a bit different. It has been published to coin-
ide with the De La Warr Pavilion's exhibition of the
ame name (on show until the end of the month at
he seaside gallery) but resolutely defines itself as
omething other than just an exhibition catalogue.
ndeed, the format and contents support this stance
no glossy image reproductions and coffee-table pro-
ortions here, but rather a series of often personal,
lways interesting pieces of writing by Beuys admir-
rs and aficionados from the art world including
acita Dean, Anthony d'Offay, Hans Ulrich Obrist and
ichard Wentworth. One for the hardcore fans rather
han Beuys novices.

n last month's book reviews Grafik warned readers about the untrust-
orthiness of books with round corners. Lo and behold, this month up
owls a publication that manages to be linen-bound, have rounded cor-
ers and be actually rather good. The House of Hardy Amies is something
f a Savile Row institution, but Amies himself was probably most famous
or being the Queen's official dressmaker, responsible for most of her
andy-coloured daywear confections until he retired in 1989. This is
ctually a reprint of book that was first published in 1964, in which
mies dishes out no-nonsense sartorial advice to a generation of young
en. Described as being "a wonderful snob with a wicked sense of humour",
s well as giving much informative advice on clothes and how to wear
hem, the author offers up some real gems here. Check out Amies's dead-
an views on everything from coathangers ("Your suit's best friend") to
ummerbunds ("A sash or a girdle worn round the waist") Need I say more?
ssential reading for any man (or woman) who would rather die than be
otted in a pair of jogging bottoms in Sainsbury's.

ostalgia is a terrible thing. It means that you look on certain things with fondness, and
ot the disdain that they clearly deserve. It means that you look at this book of fash-
on photographs and start thinking that the 80s/90s period that are covered are actually
ooking almost good again. Some of the fashion moments here may be worth resurrecting
the tailoring, silhouettes and attitude are very cool; however, the bushy eyebrows, Pat
utcher earrings, bubble perms and hideous knitwear are not. New York and Munich-based
hotographer Michael Doster is no Helmut Newton (no bad thing), and these photographs
re as much about showing off the clothes as showing off with the art direction. Like the
ashions themselves, some of the shots have aged better than others, but there's a sense
f humour present that's lacking in much fashion photography of late (and you'd definitely
eed a GSOH to wear the jewel-encrusted Joan Collinsesque King of Siam oufit featured on
he DPS). It's nicely produced and, all in all, an immensely enjoyable romp through the

One of the earliest type specimens in the collection that has been gathered in this absorbing book is by William Caslon. It was his first, for a font he designed for the Society for the Propagation of Christian Knowledge, which was destined for use in a Bible in Arabic. Being a canny marketer, Caslon made a specimen to try to sell the font to other printers. Other highlights include picture fonts of animals and clothing from the 1890s, and some French ornaments from 1900 and magnificent Spanish typefaces for missals from 1799. As this rich collection shows, specimens give us a fantastic visual history of the development of typeface design. The collector's tastes tend slightly towards the florid and pastoral but there is plenty of inspiring type here (beautifully reproduced across 360 large-format pages) to occupy even a casual type enthusiast. There is also a special code unique to each copy that gives you online access to over 1,000 digital scans, making this book a snip at twice the price. We can't wait for volume two.

**Type: A Visual History of Typefaces and Graphic Styles** (Volume One, 1628–1900) Published by Taschen, £34.99

Let's start by clearing up any confusion among non-tat aficionados: the 'flash' that is being referred to here is not the Adobe software pro-gramme, but the original outline of a design that is traced to form the basis of your average tattoo. This book looks at the artwork of artists who might be best known for their tattoo work, but have now branched out into more traditional ways of presenting their work (in galleries, on walls and on the odd skateboard). As you'd imagine, many of the art-ists featured retain the motifs and styles of the traditional tattoo genre — there are roses, dragons, snakes and skulls aplenty. Add a nice sprinkling of gothic weirdness and you pretty much get the idea about the contents of this book. Some of the artists are more accomplished than others, but, like the tattoos themselves, most of it is a bit of an acquired taste. But then maybe if you're happy to have the likes of Axl Rose or the Grim Reaper permanently etched onto your body, you probably won't object that much to having them hung on your wall.

**Art by Tattooists Beyond Flash** By Jo Waterhouse Published by Laurence King, £12.95

All too often with design books you feel like you are holding something that's been churned out by a profit-seeking publishing company. We've nothing against making money from books but following formulas and skimping on quality simply to fill a niche in the market doesn't give us a warm glow. A very hearty wel-come, then, goes to a book like We Are the Friction, a genuinely brilliant idea, extremely well executed by independent publishers. The diminutive but packed paperback is the work of Jez Burrows and Lizzie Stew-art of Sing Statistics in Edinburgh. They have teamed twelve illustrators with twelve writers to produce original works — the first half being "stories from illustrations", the second half "illustrations from stories". The experiment offers a fascinating insight into the creative process of writing and illustrat-ing. What is it in a story that sparks the idea for how to sum it up in a drawing? And how do writers' imaginations take flight in response to visual works? A glimpse of the answer is here. You can purchase your copy from Analogue Books in Edinburgh or by visiting www.singstatistics.co.uk.

**We Are the Friction: Illustration vs. Short Fiction** Published by Sing Statistics, £12.00

WE ARE THE FRICTION
ART BY TATTOOISTS
ILLUSTRATION VS. SHORT FICTION Jo Waterhouse
EDITED BY SING STATISTICS
80s/90s
TASCHEN
DAMIANI

**Polish Posters 1945-89**
Museum of Modern Art,
NYC, 11 West 53rd Street
Reviewed by BUZZ POOLE

Tucked into a corner of the MoMA's Architecture and Design Gallery, Polish Posters 1945–89 falls under the umbrella of a larger multidisciplinary exhibit called Rough Cut, which focuses on design that results from "radical engagement with form and emotion". These posters emphasise what can be achieved when designers work under great political and cultural unrest. Yes, this work is commercial and the commissioning of these posters, most of which promote cultural events, was sponsored by the state. But most of these graphic creations were made with the intention of subverting the state. The exhibit's literature explains: "Poland maintained the most consistent and broad-based resistance to Soviet control... and hostility to the Communist party and the regime was never far below the surface."

Take, for instance, Policja (The Police), Mieczyslaw Gorowski's 1982 illustration of a noose that threads through a man's eyes, ears and mouth, rendered for the production of a play; it speaks directly to the martial law imposed in Poland in December 1981 in an effort to thwart the first non-Communist trade union. Unable to see, hear or speak, the figure implies how the Polish police were at once victimisers and the victims.

The predicament of such a double bind born out of the post-war era is a theme running through many of these works. Marcin Stajewski's poster for a dramatisation of War and Peace relies on the brutal imagery of a white dove, its beak bloodied by a self-inflicted wound that flares out of the bird's breast. Macbeth's head, as conceived by Andrzej Pagowski, is wrapped in a brick crown of psychic entrapment, evoking the plot of this play and the tragedy of prophecy fulfilled; the wall fortifies Macbeth from the enemy and from himself.

Examples of humour and whimsy do exist, however, as in Maciej Urbaniec's Cyrk (Circus) in which the Mona Lisa, for no apparent reason, has been put under the big top, her iconic torso enhanced by leotard-clad legs bent up over her head in a rubbery contortion. Cul-de-sac, Roman Polanski's films about American mobsters on the lam who hide out in an isolated castle and kill time by toying with a sexually eccentric couple (he's a transvestite, she's a nymphomaniac), receives a blocky treatment from designer Jan Lenica; the black figures, a red heart and cobalt lettering favour primal simplicity over insinuated complexity.

In the wake of the war and the ensuing Communist influence, these designers were liberated from convention by virtue of reeling from the horrors of everyday life in Poland, resulting in the creation of so many wonderfully ghastly posters comprised of expressive colouring and forms. The ideological tug of war between reality and the potential of reality is present throughout, making for designs that are immediately recognisable, and timeless.

Poster for STU's premiere of Leszek Moczulski's alternative theatre production of Exodus, 1974, by Jan Sawka, (born 1947), offset lithograph. Courtesy The Museum of Modern Art.

STU
THEATRE

EXODUS

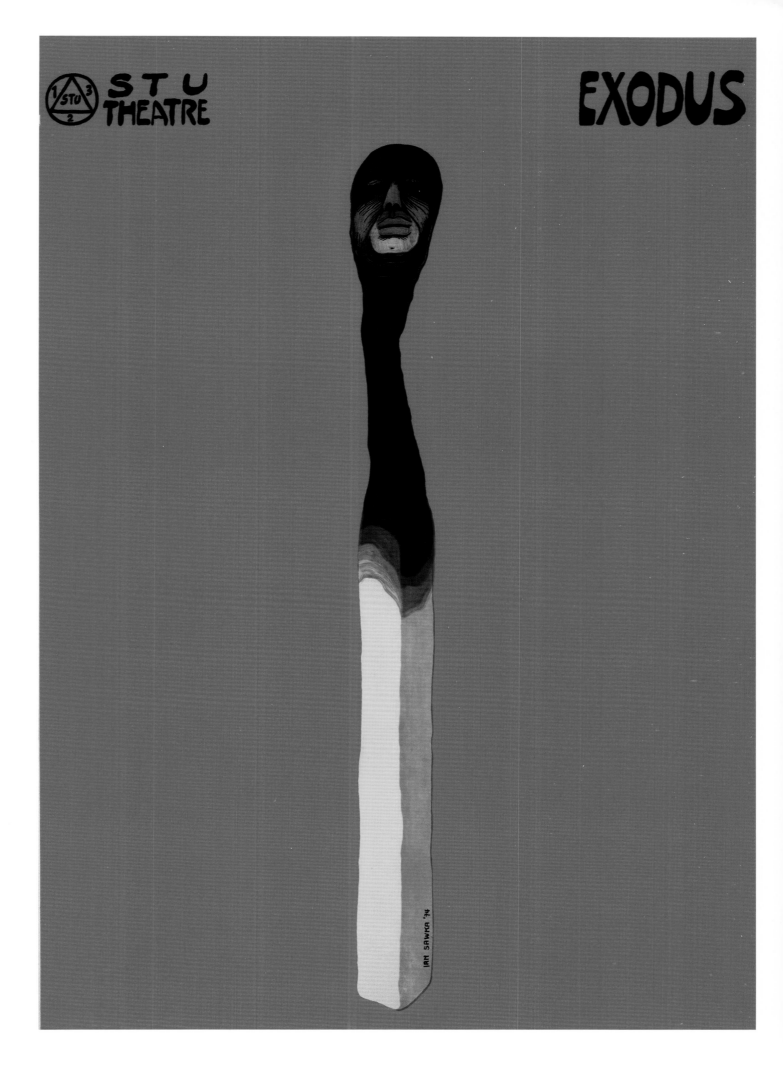

Performance of Brian
Eno's Apollo (1983),
in a new live
arrangement by
Woojun Lee,
played by Icebreaker
and BJ Cole
Science Museum, 20
and 21 July 2009
Reviewed by MAX
LEONARD

Walking through the Science Museum, you encounter the two contrary faces of space travel. Grounded in one gallery is the actual Apollo 10 command module. A squat, primitive piece of technology, well suited to the serious business of crashing to Earth, it is shaped like a stoppered flask from a school science lab. Its underside is scorched, despite the Teflon coating (NASA's best invention?) that protected it from the fiery re-entry into the atmosphere. It is corporeal, terrestrial; visibly, it has gravity. At the gallery's other end perches a replica of the Apollo 11 lunar module that ferried Armstrong and Aldrin to the greyscale surface of the moon. It is pure function – yet, being built for unknowable conditions, it is also ethereal, almost nonsensical. A Blue Peter-esque concoction of a craft that could surely never have existed. We've been to Button Moon, we've followed Mr Spoon…

Apollo 11 mission badge, 1969.
Courtesy SSPL/Nasa

The crowning contradiction of the Apollo programme is that it achieved something so momentous, was such a leap of the imagination, that it is frankly unbelievable. If you are inclined towards doubt, none of the evidence on display will convince you the Moon landings really took place. Nor could the footage from Al Reinert's film To All Mankind as it was shown on the Science Museum's IMAX screen – accompanied by a live performance of a new arrangement of Brian Eno's Apollo album. The film recounts the story of Apollo, from JFK's vision to splashdown in the Pacific. It documents the Cold War imperative to flex capitalism's muscles, but also an idealism tempered with narcissism – we are turning the camera on ourselves, from the outside, for the first time.

Space flight freed humankind from gravity and Eno worked similarly with music. His soundtrack accentuates the power and grace of the rockets, and the ominous peace of space, disorienting and vertiginous, the astronauts tiny and so vulnerable. This is serious business: lines of worry mark men's faces in Mission Control as they push buttons and study parabolas arcing across giant screens. Science, here, is faith: they must blindly believe that the equations written on the blackboard still obtain 200,000 miles away, or else we are lost. Michael Collins has spoken of his mortal terror that his crewmates, Buzz and Neil, would become stranded on the Moon, suffocate, and he would return to Earth a pariah, dreadfully alone. Planet Earth is blue and there's nothing I can do…

Yet there is also levity. Moonwalkers — space tourists — pose for photos next to the American flag, bounce around and fall over like absurd, ungainly babies learning to walk. One drops a rock sample from his shovel, replaces it and continues, for all the world like a child in an egg-and-spoon race. They are innocents, before the shock of returning from the void, their Fall. They exhibit a naïve, frontier bravery that is difficult now to imagine. Eno chose the pedal steel guitar, he says, because all but one Apollo astronaut chose to take country music with them. Some people call me the Space Cowboy…

These performances helped to restore a sense of wonder to space travel for generations since grown accustomed to having everything at the touch of a button; 400,000 people working for a decade to achieve something incredible. NASA plans to put more people up there, but somehow it feels like we can never go back.

**Art and Text**
Published by Black Dog
Reviewed by
ROBERT URQUHART

Ceci n'est pas une critique. It's statements like that — I'm thinking about your pipe here, Mr Magritte — that will go getting art a bad name. How I wish that conversation had happened in 1928. This art of the blindingly obvious has become a prevalent force in contemporary art, and Art and Text delves into that foggy world with gusto, delivering a thought-provoking read with plenty of nice big images to skim through. Unfortunately the kind of thoughts that provoked this writer were of the knee-jerk Daily Mail variety — I found myself shouting "that's not art" at the book. It turns out I'm an absolute philistine at heart. Damn.

After a truly impenetrable foreword (perhaps because the type is kerned so tight) things liven up a bit with essays by Will Hill, Charles Harrison and Dave Beech. We then crack on to the images, of which there are many, divided up into four fields: text, context, semiotext and textuality.

The subject matter and artist grouping is completely valid and will be of interest to any-one who has more than a passing interest in contemporary art. It's as accessible as this kind of conceptual art gets (which in my book is not very accessible). As Art and Text says, "the use of written language has been one of the most defining developments in vis-ual art of the twentieth century." I agree, but oh dear me, isn't that a cop-out? Isn't it somehow cheating to whack up a sentence in neon and call it art? (Pure Daily Mail, please forgive me).

Isn't this all about artists playing at being graphic designers, social anthropologists and politicians? Was it the addition of text to art what killed art and gave birth to a string of B-list cultural pariahs, dabbling in other creative fields while protecting their shoddy output in a shroud labelled 'art'?

All the usual suspects get a look in: Kurt Schitters Jeremy Duller, Bar-bara Kruger, Martin Creed, Simon Patterson, Bob & Roberta Smith and — my all-time pet hate, simply for having too much time on their hands — The Guerrilla Girls. But there are some great new additions. My knowledge of contemporary art stops abruptly when I walked away from the fine art world, disgusted at the greed, hypocrisy and arrogance of the industry in 2003, so I'm pleased to see newer works on display including a great piece called Us World Studies II by Jules De Balincourt from 2005, which takes pride of place on the centrefold. (I'm not that damaged, then).

I don't hate this book, I just hate the subject. It's a great compendium of culprits really. I would have loved it when I was a fresh-faced art student; heck, I'd even like it as a present now, something to get me shouting when I'm constipated. If you like your art with a textual feeling then it will be sure to get you in the mood.

Barbara Kruger, Untitled (Don't turn me inside out), 2008. Courtesy Mary Boone Gallery, New York.

DON'T TURN ME INSIDE OUT

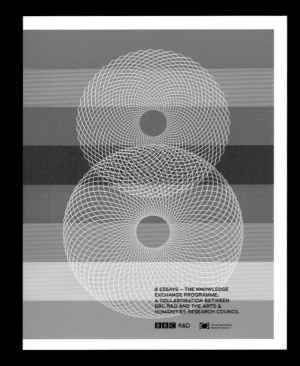

Cover of 8 Essays, a new
publication for the BBC
by Newspaper Club

Things our friends
have written on the
internet, 2008
Newspaper Club
The Revival Network
Reviewed by
MICHAEL BOJKOWSKI

Recessions, downturns, crunches — whatever you want
to call them — are boom times for creative thinking.
Innovation becomes the key to keeping going. Nowhere
is this more evident than in the field of printed
media and the newly humbled newspaper. Whereas in
the States the closure of a number of local papers
has led to widespread panic reaching all the way to
the upper echelons of the New York Times, in the UK
papers like the Guardian have resigned themselves to
the fact that their current presses may well be the
last they buy and are fully embracing multi-channel
communications.

None of this recent 'turmoil' seems to have signalled the end of newsprint as a medium. Indeed, designers in particular seem to have picked
up the baton. It makes a lot of sense when you consider the scale you can
achieve for comparatively little cost, the downsides being its longevity
(or rather the lack thereof) and getting inky fingers. There's a certain
affection for newsprint too, as exemplified in the ideas behind Newspaper Club and The Revival Network. Both projects seek to revive localised
news through magazine-style editorial and bright, full-colour artwork.

Newspaper Club was born out of a one-off publishing experiment called Things Our Friends
Have Written on the Internet 2008. TOFHWOTI did what it says on the tin, i.e., gathered a
bunch of articles and tweets from various blogs and sites, laid them out and then rolled
the presses. A limited run of 1,000 copies were sent to friends and the curious. It was
designed and produced by the Really Interesting Group, who then went on to set up Newspaper Club, a service offering bespoke newsprint publications. The first Newspaper Club
project has just been produced for the BBC, with its next project, for Penguin, already
under way.

The Revival Network was set up by Dylan at Unequal-Design
to help anyone looking to bolster their local news media.
The Revival Network site offers templates, how-tos and
loads of useful information for would-be journalists and
amateur designers. Dylan even went so far as to take his
own advice and produce The Citizen—Cheyenne, for and by
the people of Cheyenne, Wyoming. The Revival Network site
continues to provide up-to-date information on the state
of newsprint media around the world.

Obvious examples of this newsprint renaissance include Spin's self-
published journals, which started life as a piece of self-promotion
and have mutated into topical musings on graphic design through the
ages; when Special Ten relaunched as File magazine, art directors Fabio
Sebastinelli and Thorbjørn Ankerstjerne wrapped a high-quality cover
around a lower grade newsprint interior; Won is a freesheet that focuses
on photography bringing the preserve of coffee-table books to street
level; Graphic Thought Facility took the unwieldy broadsheet format and
produced a catalogue/magazine for Tom Dixon, making use of sprawling
illustrations by Jamie McLellan. Look around and you'll find even more
examples. Newspapers may be dying a slow death but the popularity of
newsprint marches on.

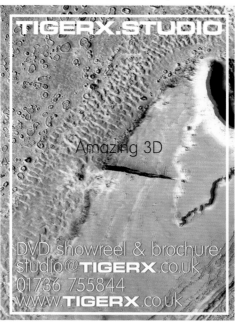

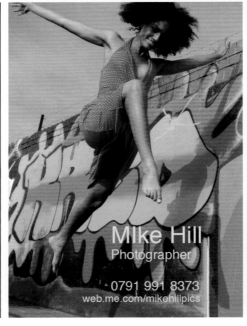

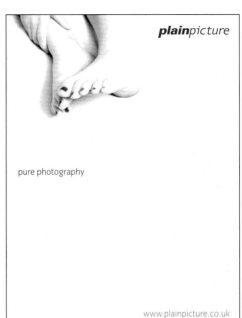

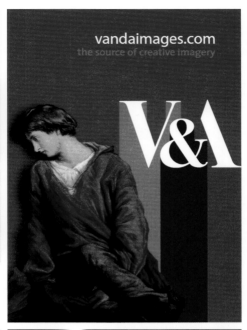

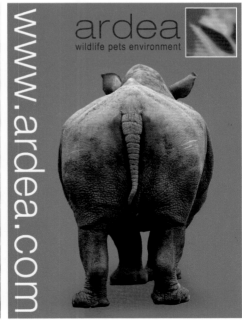

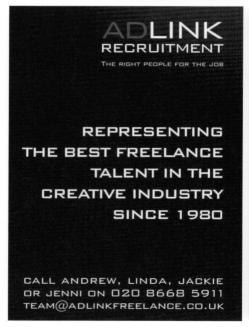

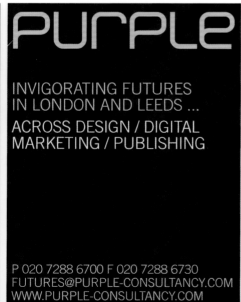

# Typography

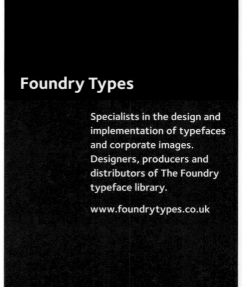

# Print & Packaging

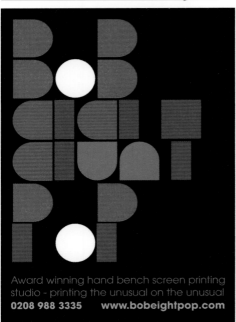

## PRINTING

TEAM IMPRESSION
+44 (0)113 272 4800
www.team-impression.com

## PAPER

Arctic Volume by
Arctic Paper
www.arcticpaper.com

Supplied by
Howard Smith Paper
www.hspg.com

## TYPEFACES

Neuzeit and Lettera
www.linotype.com
www.lineto.com

## EDITORIAL

Publisher and Editor-in-Chief
CAROLINE ROBERTS
caroline@grafikmagazine.co.uk

Editor
ANGHARAD LEWIS
angharad@grafikmagazine.co.uk

Senior Reporter
ROBERT URQUHART
robert@grafikmagazine.co.uk

Sub-Editor
ROBERT SHORE

Studio Assistant
THOMAS MOULD
thomas@grafikmagazine.co.uk

## DESIGN

Designer and Art Director
MATILDA SAXOW
matilda@grafikmagazine.co.uk

Design Assistant
A YOUNG KIM
a-young@grafikmagazine.co.uk

## GRAFIK MAGAZINE

Third Floor
104 Great Portland Street
London W1W 6PE, UK
+44 (0) 20 7637 5900
hello@grafikmagazine.co.uk
www.grafikmag.com

## COMMERCIAL

Sales Director
STEFAN KETELSEN
stefan@grafikmagazine.co.uk
+44 (0)7876 798 762

Marketing Manager
NICOLE TOWNSIN
nicole@grafikmagazine.co.uk
+44 (0)20 7637 5900

## PRODUCTION / WEB

Production Manager
and Deputy Web Editor
DAN ROLFE JOHNSON
dan@grafikmagazine.co.uk

## DISTRIBUTION

ADAM LONG
+44 (0)7961 007 139

## SUBSCRIBE

+44 (0)1635 588 498
grafik@circdata.com
www.grafikmag.com

## BUY

Grafik is sold on
newsstands worldwide and
in your local branch of
WH Smith, Borders,
Waterstones, Barnes & Noble
and other good retailers

## PUBLISHING

Grafik is published twelve
times a year by Adventures
in Publishing Ltd
ISSN no. 1479-7534